WITHDRAWN

At Issue

Are Teen Curfews Effective?

Other Books in the At Issue Series:

At Issue

Are Teen Curfews Effective?

Roman Espejo, Book Editor

GREENHAVEN PRESS
A part of Gale, Cengage Learning

GALE
CENGAGE Learning™

Detroit • New York • San Francisco • New Haven, Conn • Waterville, Maine • London

Christine Nasso, *Publisher*
Elizabeth Des Chenes, *Managing Editor*

For more information, contact:
Greenhaven Press
27500 Drake Rd.
Farmington Hills, MI 48331-3535
Or you can visit our Internet site at gale.cengage.com

Articles in Greenhaven Press anthologies are often edited for length to meet page requirements. In addition, original titles of these works are changed to clearly present the main thesis and to explicitly indicate the author's opinion. Every effort is made to ensure that Greenhaven Press accurately reflects the original intent of the authors. Every effort has been made to trace the owners of copyrighted material.

Cover image ©Images.com/Corbis.

LIBRARY OF CONGRESS CATALOGING-IN-PUBLICATION DATA

Are teen curfews effective? / Roman Espejo, editor.
    p. cm. -- (At issue)
Includes bibliographical references and index.
ISBN-13: 978-0-7377-4284-8 (hardcover)
ISBN-13: 978-0-7377-4283-1 (pbk.)
1. Youth curfews--United States--Juvenile literature. I. Espejo, Roman, 1977-
HV9104.A823 2009
364.36--dc22
                                                                    2009009478

Printed in the United States of America
1 2 3 4 5 6 7 13 12 11 10 09

Contents

Introduction

According to a 2005 poll conducted by the National League of Cities (NLC), 93 percent of the 436 communities surveyed with teen curfews believe that these laws are "very to somewhat effective" in deterring juvenile crime, while 96 percent uphold that curfew enforcement is "a good use of police officers' time." Donald J. Borut, executive director of NLC, states that "Local officials are relying on youth curfews as one way to ensure the safety of the citizens in their communities." Because of budget and federal aid cutbacks nationwide, Borut proposes, "The findings of this poll show that enhanced officer training and creative partnerships are common elements in local programs aimed at reinforcing youth curfews." Furthermore, NLC's poll shows that more communities are resorting to curfews: 67 percent that impose curfews enacted them over the past two decades, with 38 percent between 1995 and 2005.

Perhaps to the chagrin of the red-blooded American teenager, curfews are also commonplace in the nation's households. Margaret Saragrese, coauthor of *The Roller-Coaster Years*, says that in a survey of 1,000 thirteen- to seventeen-year-olds, 71 percent concede that their parents or legal guardians set curfews, and 75 percent of these teenagers support the rule. In addition, many young people eighteen and older who live at home must also abide by household curfews. For example, college student Jennifer Morron, who lives in New York city, says that she follows a curfew despite her age. "Me, I've had the same curfew since I was sixteen," she says, explaining that she still has "to be home by midnight at the latest." Observing that not all her peers have these rules, Morron remarks, "My friends think my mother is way too strict."

Household curfews are a point of contention—a part of the growing pains—between young people who desire more independence and their cautious, protective parents. But teen curfew laws, which differ in severity from city to city, are an issue of debate between members of the community, city council officials, and law enforcement agencies. For opponents, teen curfew laws are a form of bias aimed at young adults. Alex Koroknay-Palicz, executive director of the National Youth Rights Association declares, "We see it as age discrimination. . . . To think that in a free country you can be arrested for just walking down the street." David McGuire, staff attorney for the American Civil Liberties Union, Connecticut, echoes this assertion:

> Curfews, at their core, essentially place all persons of a particular demographic under "house arrest" for the actions of a minority. A curfew criminalizes all youth, regardless of whether they are breaking any laws or posing any threat. The proper response to juvenile crime is instead to arrest the criminals.

Nonetheless, supporters—including many teenagers—contend that teen curfews are needed to promote the safety of neighborhoods. In *USA Weekend* magazine's tenth annual survey on teens and their freedom, 50 percent of young people report that they support the enforcement of teen curfews for their protection and welfare. Respondent Brandi Yasuoka says, "I totally agree with adults wanting to step up laws to protect millions of minors . . . [T]eens have to prove that they can control themselves." A CBS News/*New York Times* poll also shows that parents overwhelmingly back teen curfew laws by 87 percent. Moreover, when teen curfews were enacted in such major cities as San Diego, Dallas, and New Orleans, juvenile crime fell by at least 20 percent.

As teen curfews—including daytime curfews, mall curfews, and driving curfews—place more restrictions on teenagers, the issue of whether they serve the best interest of young people and communities will continue to be contested. Reflecting upon her friends' looser curfews and the genuine concerns of parents, Morron speculates, "Although I envy most of my girl-friends who do not have to be home until 2 or 3 P.M., I often think about them and wonder, 'Do their parents realize that their daughters are out that late?'" In *At Issue: Are Teen Curfews Effective?*, the authors present a wide range of views on how well curfew laws address truancy, delinquency, and juvenile crime and instill adolescents with a sense of responsibility and communities with a sense of security.

1

Teen Curfews Create a Sense of Safety

Patrick Boyle

Patrick Boyle is editor of Youth Today, *a national newspaper for youth service professionals.*

The few scientific studies on age-based curfews demonstrate that they have little to no effect on juvenile crime or victimization. In addition, many towns and cities do not have the data to support claims that juvenile crime is on the rise. However, a growing number of communities across the United States are adopting curfews, and a recent national survey shows that local officials widely support them. The drive of policy makers to impose curfews is not about studies or data—it is about a community's impression of juvenile delinquency and crime, in which anecdotal evidence is gathered from neighbors, the local news media, and personal observations or experiences. To these people, curfews are reasonable and successful when they contribute to a feeling of safety in the community.

As head of the Center on Juvenile and Criminal Justice, Dan Macallair has repeatedly given city officials scientific data that juvenile curfews don't reduce youth crime. That evidence includes a study he co-authored, which appears to be the most comprehensive research ever done on the subject.

But Macallair can't compete with Lerrel Marshmon. Last year [2005], Marshmon appeared before the town council of

Patrick Boyle, "Curfews and Crime," *Youth Today*, November 2006, p. 36–38. Copyright © 2008 *Youth Today*, published by the American Youth Work Center. Reproduced by permission.

Knightdale, N.C., urging it to impose a curfew. The minutes of the meeting summarize his evidence:

"Lerrel Marshmon, 308 Laurens Way, Knightdale, stated that he gets off work at 10:00 P.M. and frequently the gang members come onto his property. He stated that the kids verbalized swear words to his wife. Mr. Marshmon stated that he came outside to ask the kids to leave his property and they threatened him and his family. He explained that he thinks the problem is very serious."

Among more than 200 cities with curfews, officials in 96 percent consider them "very" or "somewhat" effective.

Macallair says that when he gives officials his evidence about curfews, he usually gets "no response." After Marshmon and others spoke in Knightdale, the town instituted a curfew, and this summer decided not to change it. Knightdale is among numerous communities that have recently turned to curfews to crack down on an alleged rise in juvenile crime. San Francisco, Houston, Washington, Oklahoma City, New Haven, Conn., Kinston, N.C., and the New York communities of Rochester, Oswego, Fulton, East Syracuse and Wyoming County—those are just some of the places that have created, expanded, restored or considered curfews over the past several months [of 2006].

This despite the fact that research shows little or no evidence that curfews work. And the rise in juvenile crime? In many if not most of the towns, there's no data to support the claim.

While it's routine to bemoan the gap between research and practice in youth work, perhaps nowhere is that gap wider than between the popularity of youth curfews and the research about their effectiveness.

"What's most astounding," Macallair says about the research, "is that it's one of those areas where there doesn't seem to be any relationship whatsoever to policy analysis."

Indeed, a survey released this year [2006] by the National League of Cities shows that among more than 200 cities with curfews, officials in 96 percent consider them "very" or "somewhat" effective. The headline on the league's news release: "Youth Curfews Continue to Show Promise."

The league called curfews "a growing trend."

If curfews are demonstrably ineffective, are all those mayors, county supervisors and police chiefs ignorant, deceitful or out of their minds?

The bugaboo of the youth field about lack of research dissemination is one culprit. Officials considering curfews typically don't know about the work of Macallair and others.

But it probably wouldn't matter. While advocates who oppose curfews think their data make for a slam-dunk case, policymakers aren't impressed; they have other factors on their minds.

Data Do Not Matter

"Whereas, the town council has determined that there has been an increase in juvenile violence, juvenile gang activity and crime by persons under the age of 18 . . ."

So begins the ordinance that created the curfew in Knightdale (pop.: 6,000). But ask Police Chief Ricky Pope for data to back up the statement, and he says he probably has none. "It really wasn't because juvenile crime was up," he says of the curfew.

The answers are similar around the country. While officials justify curfews with claims about increases in youth crime, few can provide statistics to show it.

The city of Oswego, N.Y., is considering a youth curfew, but the main curfew proponent hasn't asked the police department for juvenile crime numbers. "If they have it, we don't get it," says Councilwoman Barbara Donahue. Oklahoma City expanded the hours of its youth curfew in August [2006] for its popular nightlife section, Bricktown, after business owners said youth crime and gang activity were rising there. City police say they have no juvenile crime statistics for Bricktown.

In Kinston, N.C.—which instituted a trial curfew in June and made it permanent in September [2006]—Councilman Van Broxton voted for the measure, but says, "I don't know that we had a lot of criminal data."

Even when data are provided, the conclusions are debatable:

- Police statistics from Rochester, N.Y., show juvenile arrests virtually unchanged from 2004 to 2005 (1,526 vs. 1,523). Arrests increased during the first five months of this year [2006], then dropped sharply for three months—the three months immediately preceding the city's new curfew. When the curfew began on Sept. 5 [2006], the number of juvenile arrests for the first eight months of the year was down by 6 percent from the same period last year [2005]. (After the curfew, however, the arrests fell even faster.)

- In San Francisco, the mayor announced in September [2006] that the city would begin enforcing its long-ignored curfew for anyone under 14, in response to an increase in overall violent crime. City statistics show that juvenile arrest rates declined significantly over the past decade but rose slightly from 2004 to 2005. They also show that youth under 14 make up a small percentage of those detained in the city's juvenile hall—8.4 percent last year [2005], and 6.4 percent through August of this year [2006].

- Perhaps the strongest statistics came from Washington, D.C., which extended the hours of its curfew this summer in response to what it called a crime emergency. Among other things, police cited an 82 percent increase in juvenile robberies.

Jason Ziedenberg, executive director of the Washington-based Justice Policy Institute, sat before the city council and demonstrated the futility of fighting curfews with data. He argued that the city's crime increase was driven by adult crime. He argued that the juvenile robbery totals were so small (rising from 70 to 134) that large jumps in percentages were misleading. While police said the curfew reduced juvenile arrests by 46 percent, Ziedenberg countered with an analysis which said that over 23 days, the new curfew rules reduced arrests from 15 to 13. When he was done, "there wasn't a single word from any councilor about my testimony," Ziedenberg recalls. He even asked one of them if he had any questions, "and there was no comment."

The curfews show how a community's belief about crime—based on what residents see and talk about among themselves, and what the news media and government officials report—speak louder than spreadsheets.

Impressions Drive Policy

The evidence that has driven policymakers to impose curfews this year [2006] is primarily not about data; it's impressionistic.

"It really wasn't because juvenile crime was up," the Knightdale police chief says of the curfew there. "Our problem was we were having groups of people, juveniles, hanging out in different locations and pretty much harassing the public as they walk down the sidewalk." There also seemed to be more graffiti.

The story is similar in Oswego, where some of the concerns clearly involve youth, while others involve youth by implication.

Residents have been complaining about "young people ... demanding money, using obscenities, throwing eggs at cars," Councilwoman Donahue says. "They're out here at 11 o'clock right to three or four o'clock in the morning. I've seen them myself."

She says there's been more vandalism, including to a Little League concession stand and a city pool. She adds that town officials have been hearing more from "homeowners with their cars being broken into. Cars keyed, rifled through." She says it happened to her daughter-in-law.

How does she know the culprits are kids? "You can tell just by the loose change," Donahue says, noting that the perpetrators seem more intent on being a nuisance than on finding valuables. "I don't think an adult would take and throw stuff all over the place. . . . An adult would probably just take what they need and leave."

In some towns a few serious, high-profile crimes are behind the curfews. Rochester imposed its curfew in September [2006] because of what the *Rochester Democrat and Chronicle* called "a spate of violence involving youths last year [2005] that has continued this year." The city reported that seven youths (ages 12 to 17) were killed in 2005; the curfew idea gained momentum after a 15-year-old was shot to death outside a recreation center one night last fall [in 2005]. In New Haven, Conn., a flurry of violence this summer [2006]—including the shooting deaths of three teens—[had] officials considering a curfew. A city alderwoman also cited kids on bicycles stirring up trouble in her neighborhood.

To be sure, arrest data are not a perfect reflection of criminal activity in a community; vandals routinely get away. And some of the quality-of-life issues that residents complain about, such as being shouted at by teens, often don't lend themselves to arrests.

The curfews show how a community's belief about crime—based on what residents see and talk about among themselves, and what the news media and government officials report—speak louder than spreadsheets.

The Spreadsheets

There are few studies about the impact of curfews, and their findings are uniform. In 2003, the Urban Institute released two studies of curfews in Prince George's County, Md., which borders Washington. They found "little support for the hypothesis that the curfew reduced arrests and calls for service during the curfew hours," and "little support for the hypothesis that the curfew reduced violent victimization of youth within the curfew age." The studies were funded by the National Institute of Justice.

Prince George's County still has a youth curfew.

The largest curfew study looked at California, including jurisdictions with and without curfews. Conducted by the Justice Policy Institute with funding from The California Wellness Foundation, the study looked at youth arrest and crime rates from 1978 through 1996, and was published in 1998.

The main finding: "No evidence that curfews reduce the rate of juvenile crime." Counties with strict curfews saw no decrease in crime compared with counties without strict curfews. Macallair compiled the study with researcher Mike Males (who is also a *Youth Today* columnist).

So what?

In Oswego, Councilwoman Donahue says no one has talked about finding studies about the impacts of curfews, although a curfew committee might do that.

Asked if Knightdale looked at studies about the effects of curfews elsewhere, Police Chief Pope says, "No." And they don't much care. People in towns with curfews are comfortable judging their effectiveness not by data from other states, but by observations made by themselves and people they trust.

In Kinston (pop.: 24,000), the public safety chief talked with officials from other towns with curfews, who said the curfews were working, Councilman Broxton says. One such town is Knightdale, where Councilman Jeff Eddins says, "What I would have someone look at is the number of complaints that we no longer get. The number of streets you can now drive down and not have people harassing or cursing you."

That approach explains why Ziedenberg of the Justice Policy Institute says that when he gives government officials evidence that curfews don't work, "the reaction varies from stony silence to dismissal."

When it comes to curfew decisions, data are no match for feeling safe.

An Attractive Option

It's easy to see why local government officials like curfews.

"I've been on the council for six years, and there's never been an issue that brought as many people out as this issue," says Eddins in Knightdale. "From a political standpoint, it was an easy decision to make. You've got a majority of your citizens saying, 'Take action now. We want this fixed.'"

In Rochester, a local TV station (WROC) asked residents in September [2006], "Are you in favor of Rochester's youth curfew?" Eighty-eight percent said "yes."

If it were up to you, would you go against such public wishes, and stake your case on what Macallair says happened in California a decade ago?

Macallair understands why curfews seem reasonable to most people. "From a gut level, you want to have police be able to arrest kids who are out on the street after hours," he says. "If you've got kids, that makes lots of sense." It helps that police usually support the proposals. In some communities, however—such as Oswego and New Haven—police have objected to diverting their resources to chase kids home. "Police officers have enough to do right now besides baby-sit for other people's children," the president of the New Haven police union said in the *Providence Journal*. He added that a curfew would "create more hostility between our cops and the kids."

Feeling an Impact

In Knightdale, there are no data to say juvenile crime has gone down since the curfew. But Chief Pope says the measure has been a success, based on "nothing other [than] the citizens saying it's made a big difference: 'I don't feel intimidated anymore walking down the sidewalk.'"

"The result has been great," says Eddins, the councilman. "You had groups of youth gathering in the middle of the street, on sidewalks. They were cursing, making threatening gestures to families. . . .

"With the curfew, that's been eradicated. People can actually walk up and down the streets. The kids can play in the front yards."

So while studies might see no change in crime statistics, residents weigh quality-of-life issues that don't show up in the statistics. "Every time I talk to [community leaders], they tell me the same stuff: Thanks for the curfew. Their neighborhoods feel safer," Eddins says.

When it comes to curfew decisions, data are no match for feeling safe.

2

Teen Curfews Should Not Be Supported

National Youth Rights Association

*Based in Washington, D.C., the National Youth Rights Associa-
tion is the largest youth-led organization in the United States.*

*Teen curfews should be opposed on several grounds. First of all,
curfews do not reduce juvenile crime. In fact, the current available data show that these laws may actually increase crime. Second, teen curfews interfere with parenting. Parents do not need
the government to manage their households or set curfews for
their children. Finally, teen curfews violate civil rights. Though
not inherently racist, curfews are more heavily enforced in black
communities. In addition, lower courts have struck down these
laws because they restrict the exercise of free speech. Government
intervention should not be required to monitor young people's
personal activities at any given hour.*

*W*e have curfews? What are they?

Curfews usually exist only in times of national emergency
or military occupation. On June 14, 1940, when the Germans
occupied Paris, they imposed an 8 o'clock curfew. The United
States puts a new twist on this familiar concept by setting curfews during times of peace for all young people under a certain age. Curfew laws are often set by a city or a state and
make it illegal for a person underage to be outside during cer-

National Youth Rights Association, "Curfew FAQ," National Youth Rights Association
Web site, n.d. September 2008. Reproduced by permission. http://www.youthrights.org/
curfewfaq.php.

tain times. For example, in the state of Michigan, it is illegal for a person under 16 to be out in public between the hours of 12 and 6 A.M. Cities within the state often impose curfew laws with stricter requirements than the state.

What are penalties for breaking curfew?

That depends on the law; each one is different. In some cases, the police will simply give a warning, others will make the youth return home; in other cases there may be a fine or jail time involved. For example, in St. Louis, Missouri, curfew violators face up to $500 in fines and 90 days in jail. In some cases, parents face penalties when their children are out past curfew as well. In St. Louis, if a young person has been picked up for curfew and taken to the police station, the parents must pick him or her up from the station within 45 minutes or face penalties of up to $500 in fines and 90 days in jail.

What are daytime curfews?

In addition to laws that make it a crime to be outside at night, there are also laws that make it a crime to be out during the day, usually during school hours. The city of Los Angeles has a curfew making it illegal for anyone under 18 in school to be in public between the hours of 8:30 A.M. and 1:30 P.M.

Curfews don't affect crime and only hurt innocent youth—repeal them.

Does my city have a curfew?

Possibly—youth curfews are spreading in cities and states all across the country. Please visit this list [at www.youthrights.org] to see if you are included. Due to the rapid expansion of curfew laws in the last few years, our list may not be complete, but it's the best we've seen. You can help add to our list by providing us information on your cities' curfew laws.

Do curfews cut down on youth crime?

No. Supporters of youth curfews cite only anecdotal and incidental data; the only true study on the effectiveness of youth curfews at reducing crime showed it had no effect. Researchers Mike A. Males and Dan McAllister said, "Statistical analysis does not support the claim that curfew and other status enforcement reduces any type of juvenile crime, either on an absolute (raw) basis or relative to adult crime rates. The consistency of results of these three different kinds of analysis of curfew laws point to the ineffectiveness of these measures in reducing youth crime." In fact, curfew laws may even lead to increased crime: "The current available data provides no basis to the belief that curfew laws are an effective way for communities to prevent youth crime and keep young people safe. On virtually every measure, no discernable effect on juvenile crime was observed. In fact, in many jurisdictions, serious juvenile crime increased at the very time officials were [touting] the crime reduction effects of strict curfew enforcement."

Let's think about this rationally. Curfew laws are intended to stop young people from committing crimes by making them stay inside. If a person intends to commit a crime by stealing a car, vandalizing a home, or dealing drugs, why would they have any respect for another law that made it illegal to be outside? Aren't laws against auto theft, property damage, and drug dealing enough?

Curfews don't affect crime and only hurt innocent youth—repeal them.

A Family Decision

Should 5-year-olds be free to roam the street at 4 in the morning?

That's a family decision. Parents should be able to set curfews, not government. Parents know their children far better than an impersonal law and should be given the discretion to parent.

If curfew laws are repealed, kids will be more likely to defy their parents' curfews, seeing that the government no longer is concerned about this issue, right?

There are no laws against yelling in the house, running with scissors, or pulling hair, but parents manage to handle these issues just fine. Why do parents need police to back them up when setting curfews? As the experience of Prince George's County, Maryland, shows, often parents don't even know about the curfew law. "Despite a number of public service announcements and the distribution of 40,000 brochures to middle- and high-school students to educate them about the curfew, awareness of the curfew is not universal among parents—only three in four parents of teenagers knew of it."

Curfews and Crime

Don't curfew laws help the police fight crime?

Police are split on this issue. The creation of a substantially broad crime to allow the ability to stop and question all individuals under a certain age is a tool for police, and a way to get around individual rights. Many other officers, however, feel curfew laws create a drain on police time and resources, forcing them not only to serve and protect, but also to parent. With murderers and rapists loose on the street, making sure Billy isn't out to late should not be a police priority.

Are curfews racist?

Not inherently, but usually they turn out to be. Curfew laws give a great amount of discretion to police officers, which . . . often leads to racist enforcement of curfew laws. Curfew laws are heavily enforced in black neighborhoods, but not as much in white neighborhoods. Likewise, white youth are less likely to be stopped by police than black youth. Because of this, the rate of arrest for blacks in 2000 was 71% higher than that for whites.

Curfew hours target the period of highest youth crime, right?

No, nighttime and daytime curfews don't cover the stretch of time most juvenile crime occurs—the afternoon. According to the FBI, "Youth between the ages of 12 and 17 are most at risk of committing violent acts and being victims between 2 P.M. and 8 P.M." These are times that no curfew laws cover.

Curfews only exist in places with high rates of juvenile crime; curfew laws aren't introduced baselessly, right?

Wrong. In response to a grisly string of murders in Manning, South Carolina, the city council proposed a youth curfew in response. The problem, however, was the criminal suspect was 37-years-old, and the proposed youth curfew would have had no effect whatsoever on the murders that shocked this small town. The experience of Manning is not unusual. Communities choose to enact curfew laws that have no problems with youth crime whatsoever. In fact, except for the elderly, juvenile crime makes up the lowest proportion of crime altogether. So if adults commit 75–90% of all crime, where is the urgent need for curfew laws to protect society from violent youth?

Don't curfew laws protect young people from being victimized by criminals; shouldn't youth be glad such laws protect them?

If young people were concerned about violent criminals, they would stay inside voluntarily; no law would be needed. This line of reasoning is only correct if applied to all people at risk of being attacked by criminals. Of course, all people are at risk of crime; if protecting innocent people from crime were a legitimate concern, then all people regardless of age would clamor for, and accept, curfews governing their lives. Would a requirement that all U.S. residents be inside by 11 P.M. free the country of all crime?

In a Free Country

Are curfew laws unconstitutional?

There have been many court challenges to curfew laws around the nation, and so far courts are split on this issue. With no U.S. Supreme Court ruling on the issue, there is no easy answer to offer. In general, lower courts recognize that curfews impose restrictions to the 1st Amendment right of free speech and have struck down many laws that impose too heavy a burden on the exercise of youth's free speech rights. These same courts will often uphold curfew laws once exceptions have been written to allow for political protests. The narrow interpretation of 1st Amendment rights is a tragedy and ultimately ignores the more pressing liberty rights at issue.

Curfew laws are also deemed to be constitutional if they serve a compelling state interest, in this case, the reduction of juvenile crime. However, as no study has shown curfews, in fact, reduce crime, this assertion is false. With no compelling state interest, NYRA [National Youth Rights Association] strongly asserts curfew laws are unconstitutional and must be struck down.

Curfew laws often have exceptions if the person is coming home from work, or in an emergency; what else would a youth want to be out at night for?

In a free country, it is not our place to decide what is appropriate for our neighbor to do or not do. Freedom doesn't require proof to justify one's decisions. If a teen wants to take a stroll and gaze at the moon, that's her decision. If a teen feels it's too hot during the day and prefers jogging at night or early in the morning, that's his decision. If a teen wants to go to the park and count blades of grass at 3 in the morning, from what harm do we suffer? Freedom is not the result of exceptions to the law; the laws are the exceptions to freedom.

What can I do to help fight curfews?

We're glad you asked. NYRA has provided for you a resource with lots of information on what you can do to fight curfews in your area. Print out stickers, start a NYRA chapter, hold a protest, and of course, let the media know. Check out NYRA's anti-curfew action site to start a campaign against your curfew. Since NYRA is one of the top organizations fighting curfews, joining the organization is a good step against curfews.

3

Teen Curfew Laws Must Respect Constitutional Rights

Pennsylvania General Assembly, Local Government Commission

The Pennsylvania General Assembly, Local Government Commission is a subcommittee of the Pennsylvania state legislature.

Teen curfew ordinances affect the personal autonomy of minors—whether religious, political, or civic—as well as the parent-child relationship. Therefore, when a municipality drafts or imposes a teen curfew, its constitutional implications must be carefully considered. A curfew must not impinge a minor's First Amendment rights, which include protected speech, such as religious and political activity. With respect to parents, a teen curfew must not interfere with a family's right to privacy and the freedom from government interference, according to the Ninth Amendment. Lastly, minors' freedom of movement and travel, as protected by the Fourteenth Amendment, must not be violated.

The common understanding of the term "curfew" is defined in *Black's Law Dictionary* as "a regulation that forbids people (or certain classes of them) from being outdoors between certain hours." The vast majority of existing municipal curfews are juvenile curfews, requiring that children of a specified age be indoors or otherwise in the presence of a guardian during night hours. According to one authority, the first juvenile curfew in the United States was enacted in 1880

Pennsylvania General Assembly, Local Government Commission, "Juvenile Curfews," *Pennsylvania Legislator's Municipal Deskbook* (3rd ed.). Harrisburg, PA: Author, September 2006, pp. 99–103. http://www.lgc.state.pa.us/deskbook06/Issues_Health_Welfare_and_Safety_04_Juvenile_Curfews.pdf.

in Omaha, Nebraska. Curfews gained prominence in the 1890s as a response to rising crime attributed to immigrant children, and according to a 1995 survey by the United States Conference of Mayors, 70 percent of 387 cities responding had curfew ordinances in place. Juvenile curfews have historically attained a similar level of prominence in Pennsylvania municipalities.

Municipalities and their solicitors should carefully research and draft curfews in a manner designed to weather any number of potential challenges, usually founded on alleged constitutional violations.

Absent a specific statutory delegation of power to enact curfews, Pennsylvania municipalities enact juvenile curfews pursuant to their general police powers for the following purposes:

- To reduce juvenile crime and thus promote the community welfare,

- To reduce perpetration of crime on juveniles that may be vulnerable during curfew hours, and

- To promote and support the parent-child relationship and provide an additional layer of supervision when appropriate.

Juvenile curfew ordinances typically have a number of characteristics in common, including an age threshold, a time period within which the regulation applies, exceptions, administrative provisions, and penalties.

While juvenile curfews in Pennsylvania are prevalent and have not been subject to an inordinate number of court challenges, municipalities and their solicitors should carefully research and draft curfews in a manner designed to weather any number of potential challenges, usually founded on alleged constitutional violations. The need for caution is based on several factors, the foremost of which is that the United States Supreme Court has yet to establish clear guidelines regarding the constitutional validity of juvenile curfews.

Furthermore, the various federal circuits that have passed on the question have established a broad spectrum of approaches. In these cases, many federal constitutional provisions have been invoked to challenge juvenile curfews.

Constitutional Implications

Curfews impact the personal autonomy of juveniles, the ability of juveniles to engage in religious, political, or civic endeavors, the relationship between parents and their children, and the arrest powers of the government. Issues involving unconstitutional vagueness may also be raised. Many of these issues may involve "fundamental rights," which are afforded great protection by the courts. Of the various constitutional provisions implicated by challenges to curfews, the following are of some prominence:

- *First Amendment Interests—Speech, Association and Expression*: Although the First Amendment to the United States Constitution has been interpreted as not providing a right to generally "socialize," it could be impermissibly infringed upon when a curfew provides no exceptions for purposes of "protected speech," such as religious or political activities. Furthermore, a curfew ordinance could be challenged as unconstitutionally overbroad when it adversely affects a substantial amount of protected activities.

- *The Ninth Amendment—the Fundamental Right of Parents to Raise Children Without Undue Interference*: The Ninth Amendment to the United States Constitution has been construed to contain a right to privacy that protects family autonomy and is related to substantive due process under the Fifth and Fourteenth Amendments. While there is disagreement in the federal circuits whether a curfew promotes or interferes with parental rights, a challenge under this amendment is more likely when a curfew ordinance prohibits activities that would be permitted or encouraged by a responsible parent.

- *Fourteenth Amendment Interests—Due Process and Equal Protection—the "Right of Locomotion"*/Freedom of Movement: To the extent that a curfew may affect interstate travel, freedom of movement, or other fundamental rights, the Fourteenth Amendment to the United States Constitution is implicated. The Equal Protection Clause of this Amendment is sometimes invoked by challengers asserting that a juvenile curfew creates an impermissible classification based on age. This Amendment is used as justification for the more rigorous "strict scrutiny" standard of judicial review when an ordinance infringes on fundamental rights.

- *"Vagueness" Issues*: Related to the guarantees of Due Process and the Fourth Amendment, an ordinance may be facially challenged on the basis of unconstitutional vagueness. This occurs where a citizen must speculate as to what constitutes a violation of the regulation, and where law enforcement officials are impermissibly delegated too much discretion as to what constitutes a violation of the regulation. *This doctrine appears to be one of the major methods by which curfew regulations are challenged.*

Drafting Municipal Curfews

Given the history of challenges to juvenile curfews both within and outside of Pennsylvania, a prudent municipality would be well-advised to prepare for a "strict scrutiny" standard to be applied to their curfew ordinance. In other words, "strict scrutiny" implies that courts will deem a curfew unconstitutional unless it "is narrowly tailored to serve a compelling governmental interest." The potential application of this standard largely stems from the fact that curfews impact the fundamental rights of minors and many federal courts have determined that those rights deserve the same level of protection as those of adults. While preventing juvenile crime and protecting juveniles generally satisfy the "compelling interest" prong of the test, a lack of a statistical basis for the curfew and exceptions that inadequately allow for the exercise of constitutional rights often cause ordinances to fail the "narrow tailoring" requirement. Furthermore, strict scrutiny demands that a sufficient "nexus" exist between the goals of the ordinance and the means used.

In reviewing a curfew ordinance, a municipality should consider, among others, the following questions:

- Can the municipality point to specific statistics that warrant the imposition of a curfew?

- Is the proposed ordinance drafted to address these issues in the least intrusive manner possible?

- Are there adequate exceptions for legitimate activities or situations that may inadvertently be unauthorized by the proposed ordinance?

- Does the proposed ordinance contain terms that are too vague?

The number of municipalities that have enacted curfews and the lack of challenges to such ordinances indicate that they remain a popular public safety tool in Pennsylvania, despite any potential constitutional difficulties. Because curfews represent a restriction on personal freedom by the state and require municipalities, in essence, to insinuate themselves in the parent/child relationship, they have sometimes been met by public resistance. As one commentator suggests, "[c]urfews place not only limitations on the activities of the two-tenths of 1 percent of youths who commit serious offenses, but also on the 99.8 percent who seek to engage in legitimate interests during nighttime hours."

4

Teen Curfew Laws
Are Unconstitutional

Spencer W. Harrington

Spencer W. Harrington is an attorney based in Washington state.

Teen curfews impinge on youths' constitutional rights and are commonly viewed as an overreaction by authorities to real or perceived increases in juvenile crime or endangerment. The First Amendment to the U.S. Constitution does not clearly express the relationship between free speech and the validity of curfews. For example, exceptions to the First Amendment, which designate the types of speech that are not protected, do not include speech by minors or speech exercised at night or any designated hours. Also, restricting minors' freedom because of children's particular vulnerability may be unconstitutional, because it is in the interest of cities to protect all citizens equally from crime. For a teen curfew to be justified, it must pass strict scrutiny—the ordinance must be narrowly tailored to meet a compelling interest of the government. In numerous cities, however, teen curfews do not exempt the constitutionally protected activities of minors and instead trample on their rights. Teen curfews, therefore, do not make sense.

Curfew—n. In places under martial law, a fixed time after which (or period during which) no citizen may remain outside. *Juvenile Curfew Ordinance*—Assigns responsibility to

Spencer W. Harrington, *The Unconstitutionality of Nocturnal Juvenile Curfews.* Spokane, WA: Lulu, 2005, pp. 2, 4–11, 14, 17–26. Reproduced by permission of the author.

the juvenile for violation of the curfew. *Parental Responsibility Ordinance*—Assigns the responsibility of a violation to the parent of the juvenile. (Some ordinances assign responsibility to both the parent and the juvenile).

Curfews have been used for over a century for a variety of purposes. There are two main types of curfews. One is in response to an emergency and the other is a non-emergency or blanket curfew. Emergency curfews are generally in response to some catastrophic event and often are accompanied by martial law. Blanket curfews are often viewed as an overreaction by authorities to real or perceived concerns and a response that unnecessarily impinges on fundamental constitutional rights. All curfews are presumed unconstitutional by the courts if enacted outside a condition of martial law. In regards to emergency curfews, this presumption of unconstitutionality has been negated when the curfew has been held a narrowly tailored means of achieving a compelling state interest. This is commonly referred to as "strict scrutiny." A blanket curfew is presumed unconstitutional. However, blanket curfews that are applied only to juveniles have received differing treatment. Some blanket juvenile curfews have been found unconstitutional and others have not. . . .

With the threat of constitutional challenges looming and the questionability of the effectiveness of juvenile curfews it just does not make sense to have a curfew. In addition, the cost associated with enforcing a curfew could be spent on supportive juvenile programs, rather than restricting juveniles. "We had to add $1 million in new police payroll to enforce our curfew" [*A Status Report on Youth Curfews in America's Cities*, United States Conference of Mayors, 1997, response by the city of San Jose, California, at http://www.usmayors.org/publications/curfew.htm]. Finally, a juvenile curfew that might be constitutional would be ineffective because there are constitutionally required exceptions that the curfew would be inapplicable to most minors. . . .

The First Amendment

The text of the First Amendment states:

> Congress shall make no law respecting an establishment of religion, or prohibiting the free exercise thereof; or abridging the freedom of speech, or of the press; or the right of the people peaceably to assemble, and to petition the Government for a redress of grievances.

First Amendment challenges in regards to juvenile curfews are based upon free speech, freedom of religion, and peaceful assembly (including the right of free movement and free association). The First Amendment is not an absolute protection for all speech. "There are certain well-defined and narrowly limited classes of speech, the prevention and punishment of which have never been thought to raise any Constitutional problem" [*Chaplinsky v. New Hampshire*, 315 U.S. 568 (1942)]. These include the lewd and obscene, the profane, the libelous, and the insulting or "fighting" words— those which by their very utterance inflict injury or tend to incite an immediate breach of the peace. There are five general categories of content-based unprotected speech; (1) Incitement, (2) Fighting Words, (3) Hostile Audiences, (4) Libel, and (5) Obscenity. If a minor or an adult were to engage in any of the prohibited speech types, this speech is accorded less or zero protection. Accordingly, a short description of each follows:

1. Incitement

The incitement exception attempts to "draw the line between 'opinion' and 'instigation'" [Sullivan & Gunther, First Amendment Law 14 (Foundation Press 1999)]. The current two-part test for incitement is (1) "where such advocacy is directed to inciting or producing imminent lawless action and (2) is likely to incite or produce such action." [*Brandenburg v. Ohio*, 395 U.S. 444 (1969)]. "The mere abstract teaching . . . of the moral propriety or even moral necessity for a resort to force and violence, is not the same as preparing a group for violent action and steeling it to such action" [*Brandenburg v. Ohio*].

2. Fighting Words

Fighting words are words that are said by the speaker and produce such a violent response in the listener that the listener is compelled to react. Thus, the violence is directed at the speaker herself, not a third party. The current definition used for fighting words is, "those which by their very utterance inflict injury or tend to incite an immediate breach of the peace" [*Chaplinsky v. New Hampshire*]. Fighting words are by definition used to produce a reaction in the listener, and are not an "essential part of any exposition of ideas, and are of such slight social value as a step to truth that any benefit that may be derived from them is clearly outweighed by the social interest in order and morality" [*Chaplinsky v. New Hampshire*].

3. Hostile Audiences

Hostile audiences are a sub-category of fighting words. The difference between fighting words and hostile audiences is that fighting words are words that themselves cause the harm. Often times fighting words are profanity and insults. Hostile audience situations arise when "an audience is provoked by either the form of the message or by the message itself" [Sullivan & Gunther].

4. Libel

Libel is the harm created by the false light shed upon a person or group by the speech or writing of another. This description is much oversimplified, and extensive analysis of libel is beyond the scope of this paper. However, libel is unprotected speech, but the test applied to libel varies with the context of the speech/press, the people involved, and the subject matter.

5. Obscenity

Obscenity is a clear content-based restriction. The First Amendment generally bars content-based censorship. The Supreme Court has placed obscenity outside the purview of the First Amendment because it is not an "essential part of any exposition of ideas, and are of such slight social value as a step to truth that any benefit that may be derived from them is clearly outweighed by the social interest in order and morality" [*Chaplinsky v. New Hampshire*].

Interestingly, none of the exceptions to free speech mention speech by minors or speech conducted during specific hours. Speech during specific hours is more likely a time and manner restriction, whereas the above-mentioned speech types are content based. If a minor were to engage in any of the above mentioned types of prohibited speech she would be subject to the same standards as an adult. However, in the case of juvenile curfews the conduct prohibited falls outside of these recognised areas of speech that are currently regulated. It is interesting that some cities believe it is ok to add an additional category of prohibited speech: speech that occurs during nighttime hours. There is no constitutional basis for such a distinction. Surely a distinction such as this would fail if applied to adults, [so] the same should be true when applied to minors. There is no distinctions in the constitutional rights of adults and minors, adults and minors have the same fundamental rights. However, the Supreme Court has allowed different treatment of minors than adults in certain circumstances. Thus, the question becomes, are minors entitled to the same First Amendment protections as adults? If not, why?

Do Minors Possess Fundamental Rights?

First Amendment rights are in the category described a "fundamental" right. It is important to first determine whether minors have the same fundamental rights as adults. "Constitutional rights do not mature and come into being magically only when one attains the state-defined age of majority." [*Planned Parenthood of Central Missouri v. Danforth*, 428 U.S. 52, 74 (1976)]. "Minors as well as adults, are protected by the Constitution and possess constitutional rights." [*Nunez v. San Diego*, 114 F.3d 935 (1997)]. "Whatever may be their precise impact, neither the Fourteenth Amendment nor the Bill of Rights is for adults alone" [*In re Gault*, 387 U.S. 1, 13 (1967)]. A child, merely because of his minority, is not beyond the protection of the Constitution. State and Federal courts have consistently recognized that juvenile curfews implicate the rights of minors.

Although minors have the same fundamental rights, some of these rights may be limited in certain specific circumstances because of their minority. Fundamental though it may be for adults, states may sometimes curtail minors' freedoms to provide them additional protection, even at the expense of their full constitutional rights. When a state has a strong interest in protecting minors, it may restrict their rights in ways in which it could not restrict adults. Nevertheless, a state's right to restrict minors' fundamental rights is not unlimited. The Supreme Court in *Bellotti v. Baird*, the leading case regarding the rights of minors, has articulated three specific factors that, when applicable, warrant differential analysis of the constitutional rights of minors and adults: (1) the peculiar vulnerability of children; (2) their inability to make critical decisions in an informed, mature manner, and (3) the importance of the parental role in child rearing.

The *Bellotti* test must be used when deciding if minors should be protected more than adults when fundamental rights are implicated. The *Bellotti* test is triggered when a fundamental right is involved. Therefore, the court must first decide whether a minor's fundamental right is involved. Once the right is determined to be fundamental, the court then examines the state conduct through a *Bellotti* lens to determine whether minors should be protected more than adults. The

Bellotti test is used to determine if the state has an adequate interest to justify the different treatment of minors from adults in a specific set of circumstances. When cities implement a juvenile curfew, most cities point to the peculiar vulnerability of children regarding crime victimization and perpetration. The Ninth Circuit, in *Nunez* [*Nunez v. San Diego*, 114 F.3d 935 (1997)], found that the interest of the city in protecting children from crime is the same as that of protecting all citizens. Additionally the court found it unexceptional that the city chose to treat a juvenile different[ly] regarding an adult during the curfew hours. However, the cities lack adequate reasons to limit a minor's freedom to be out past certain hours, the city also cannot use the curfew as justification to limit the minor's access to public forums during those hours. . . .

If a curfew did allow for broad First Amendment exceptions, it "would effectively reduce a curfew ordinance to a useless device."

Freedom of Speech Rights

The rights of freedom of speech/expression and movement implicated in a juvenile curfew are fundamental rights. The implication of these fundamental rights triggers a strict scrutiny analysis. Every court that has analyzed the right to free movement has applied a strict scrutiny analysis when applied to interstate travel. Courts are split on whether the rights to free movement are implicated in intrastate travel. . . .

First Amendment protections are important in determining the constitutionality of a curfew. Having concluded that a facial challenge is appropriate we then apply the standard three-part test to determine whether the ordinance is a reasonable time, place and manner restriction. To be a permissable time, place, and manner restriction (1) it must be content neutral, (2) it must be narrowly tailored to a significant government interest, and (3) it must leave open ample alternative channels for legitimate expression. Since the ordinances do not prohibit specific conduct and allow others it does not differentiate between types of conduct. Thus, it is usually undisputed that the regulation is content neutral.

The second prong requires the government to have a significant interest and that [the] ordinance is narrowly tailored to that interest. For First Amendment purposes the Supreme Court has recognized that "there is a compelling interest in protecting the physical and psychological well-being of minors" [*Sable Communications of California, Inc. v. FCC*, 492 U.S. 115 (1989)]. Thus, the ordinance must be narrowly tailored to achieve the physical and psychological well-being of minors. In most instances, they are not narrowly tailored because they do not sufficiently exempt lawful, innocent conduct, including First Amendment activities from the curfew. If a curfew did allow for broad First Amendment exceptions, it "would effectively reduce a curfew ordinance to a useless device" [*Nunez v. San Diego*].

The third prong of the test requires that there be ample alternative channels available. The blanket prohibition placed on minors during the curfew hours eliminates all alternative channels during those hours. The right to express oneself cannot be preserved by . . . allowing expression [only] within one's own home. In the alternative, allowing minors to express themselves during non-curfew hours is also not a legitimate alternative. In most cases allowing minors to express themselves only during non-curfew hours excludes 1/3 to 1/4 of each day. Such a broad ban excluding a large portion of every day, but allowing expressive conduct during the remainder of the day, is not a legitimate alternative.

Freedom of Movement

Another argument asserted under First Amendment challenges to juvenile curfews is that the curfew is an unconstitutional limitation on a minor's right of association. The recognized right to association is limited to (1) intimacy, and (2) "expressive association" for First Amendment activity [*City of Dallas v. Stanglin*, 490 U.S. 19 (1989)]. The right to expressive association includes assemblies for non-political purposes, such as social, legal, or economic ones, but the Constitution does not provide a generalized right to societal association outside the context of expressive association. Therefore, the minors must assert a right to expressive association that is more than a general socialization.

Many youths belong to "cliques," groups or the like, and accordingly the association with the group is part of the individual's identity. When these groups gather they are expressing their view by their language, dress, and conduct. The message of many of the groups is clear. Punk rock youths give a clear message that they are angry at society. This view is expressed through their clothing and conduct. With a group of these individuals there is no doubt that their presence sends a clear message about who they are and what they believe. This conduct, whether in an organized forum (punk rock show) or informally (hanging out) expresses a clear message. The same expressive conduct can be attributed to many other groups; cheerleaders, chess club, athletes, 4H, Young Republicans, and many others. Accordingly, the gathering of youths in public places is expressive conduct and should be accorded full protection under the First Amendment.

Citizens have a fundamental right of free movement, "historically part of the amenities of life as we have known them" [*Papachriston v. City of Jacksonville*, 405 U.S. 156, 164 (1972)]. Similarly, the Constitution guarantees the fundamental right to interstate travel. "Freedom of movement is the very essence of our free society, setting us apart. Like the right of assembly and the right of association, it often makes all other rights meaningful—knowing, studying, arguing, exploring, conversing, observing and even thinking" [*Aptheker v. Secretary of*

State, 378 U.S. 500, 520 (1964)]. This freedom is rooted both in the First Amendment's protection of association and expression and in the fundamental liberties of the Fifth Amendment. Thus, citizens have the right to travel to and from the various states. . . .

The only reason juvenile curfews exist in the absence of adult curfews is that minors lack political power and representation.

Strict Scrutiny

The designation of juvenile freedom of movement rights as a fundamental right requires the application of strict scrutiny in the analysis of juvenile curfews. If the right was less than fundamental then a lower level of scrutiny could be applied. Consequently, a lower level of scrutiny is certain to doom a juvenile curfew. Thus, it is key for the courts to recognize that minor's freedom of movement is fundamental. Some courts have upheld juvenile curfews but have not decided whether the freedom of movement rights of minors are fundamental, but still applied strict scrutiny in their analysis. Other courts have found freedom of movement to be a fundamental right of minors and struck down the curfew, also applying strict scrutiny. The Ninth Circuit is in the [latter] category.

In order to survive strict scrutiny, the classification created by the juvenile curfew ordinance must be narrowly tailored to promote a compelling governmental interest. To be narrowly tailored, there must be a sufficient nexus between the stated government interest and the classification created by the ordinance.

1. Compelling State Interest

Before a municipality can enact valid legislation which infringes on a fundamental right like freedom of movement, the government must prove a compelling need. It need not have

41

scientific or exact proof of the need for legislation. The city has a compelling interest in protecting the entire community from crime, this includes juvenile crime. The city's interest in protecting the safety and welfare of its minors is also a compelling interest.

Furthermore, the government may have a compelling interest in protecting minors from certain things that it does not for adults. Generally, in defense of a city curfew ordinance "a city claims its interest in protecting minors from the dangers of public places at night is particularly compelling, for all the reasons set forth in *Bellotti* regarding differential treatment of minors." These cities assert that greater restrictions of minors may be justified because they have a greater vulnerability at night than do adults and because minors are not equally able as adults to make mature decisions regarding the safety of themselves and others. Some courts have reached the opposite conclusion but the Ninth Circuit "agree[s] with those courts [that find] that all citizens are vulnerable to crime at night and that . . . it [is] unexceptional for the City to conclude that minors are more susceptible to the dangers of the night and are generally less equipped to deal with danger that does arise. Thus, the City may have a compelling interest in placing greater restrictions on minors than adults to insure the minors' own safety." Therefore the curfew would meet the first prong of strict scrutiny test.

2. Narrowly Tailored

"Similarly, minor curfew ordinances may be permissible where they are specific in their prohibition and necessary in curing a demonstrable social evil" [*Seattle v. Pullman*, 514 P.2d 1059 (1973)]. The question then becomes whether the ordinance is narrowly tailored to promote a compelling state interest. To be narrowly tailored, there must be an evidentiary nexus between a law's purpose and effect. . . .

Although the Constitution does not require the government to produce "scientifically certain criteria of legislation"

[*Ginsberg v. New York*, 390 U.S. 629, 642-43 (1968)], the City must "demonstrate that its classification is precisely tailored" [*Plyler v. Doe*, 457 U.S. 217 (1982)]. In general, some statistics will be more helpful than others to prove the narrow tailoring of the ordinance. . . .

If a nexus is proven to indicate that the curfew is related to the goal of reducing juvenile crime and victimization, the city must then prove that the ordinance is narrowly tailored. In order to be narrowly tailored, the ordinance must ensure that the broad curfew minimizes any burden on minors' fundamental rights, such as the right to free movement. Thus, we examine the ordinance's exceptions to determine whether they sufficiently exempt legitimate activities from the curfew. Most cities, when challenged, will argue that the ordinance has sufficient exceptions for legitimate activity. A review of the Washington ordinances shows that out of 46 ordinances only seven have comprehensive exemptions. The other 39 cities are likely enforcing an unconstitutional ordinance and trampling the rights of minors.

The seven cities that have included comprehensive exemptions in their ordinances may pass constitutional scrutiny in this one area but will still fail under the parental rights analysis, because they fail to include an exemption for parental permission. Furthermore, of these seven cities only one has an exception for intrastate travel. Thus, the other six would be subject to an intrastate travel challenge to their ordinance.

In sum, it is insufficient for a city to cite only national statistics, though these statistics may be useful when combined with local statistics ". . . but the national statistics do not conclusively show that the nocturnal juvenile curfew is a narrowly tailored solution" [*Nunez v. San Diego*]. One city cited the statistics of another city in an attempt to prove that juvenile curfews worked overall. The citing of another city's statistics has no effect on the validity of a curfew in the target city. It is also ineffective to use the "justification that the ordinance has the additional beneficial deterrent effect of permitting police officers to get juveniles off the streets before crimes are committed" [*Nunez v. San Diego*]. The Supreme Court has sharply critiqued this type of rationale as overinclusive, at least with respect to adults.

The Need Is Obsolete

Nocturnal juvenile curfews just do not make any sense. The only justification is that if we keep people in their homes that crime is less likely to occur. This is true of minors and adults. The idea of keeping all adults in at night would never be accepted, but for minors we have another standard. The only reason juvenile curfews exist in the absence of adult curfews is that minors lack political power and representation. In short, the myriad of problems that plague any juvenile curfew make implementation ineffective. This paper covered only the First Amendment challenges to juvenile curfews, but there are many other challenges as well. This accumulation of potential for litigation makes the decision to implement a curfew suspect. Furthermore, the availability of other means to combat juvenile crime and juvenile victimization make the need for a juvenile curfew obsolete.

5

Some Teen Curfew Laws Are Inconsistent

Tom Rybarczyk

Tom Rybarczyk is a former staff reporter for The Chicago Tribune.

Teen curfew laws differ from city to city and may lead to inconsistent enforcement and legal confusion for teens and their parents. Some city ordinances have been amended to protect minors' constitutional rights to engage in civic or religious activity as well as school functions, while others have not, allowing law enforcement officials to issue curfew citations before establishing whether the teen's activity is protected. Furthermore, in lieu of a 1999 court case wherein the minor obtained parental permission to stay out past curfew, parents' rights also complicate curfew enforcement.

Naperville Central High School student Jackie Dziadosz and her boyfriend, Don Lambka, were racing home from their prom in Oakbrook Terrace last month [May 2004] when a state trooper nabbed Lambka for speeding.

Already midnight when the couple left the Drury Lane, they were in violation of the Illinois curfew statute, which says anyone under 17 can't be out after 12 A.M. on weekends. Lambka, who was 16 at the time, received a curfew citation on top of his speeding ticket, forcing the pair to miss a party at a friend's home.

"[The officer] kind of ruined the prom night," said Dzia-dosz, who escaped a citation because police didn't ask for her identification.

Ironically, if Lambka had been pulled over in any number of Illinois cities and villages, he may not have been cited for missing curfew. That's because a ruling earlier this year [2004] by the U.S. Court of Appeals for the 7th Circuit struck down an Indiana curfew law on the grounds it failed to honor minors' 1st Amendment rights.

Curfew law—and its enforcement—can vary from city to city, creating a legal labyrinth for youths wishing to travel late at night.

The court's decision says police should ask minors why they are out past curfew and if they are practicing their 1st Amendment rights, such as attending a protest or a church event, police should give them a pass. The problem is, some communities have changed their law to be in line with the decision, but others are continuing their policy of ticketing first and asking questions later.

Illinois' curfew law and laws adopted by many of the state's municipalities contain the same defect as the Indiana law. So in [2004], local governments, including those in Chicago, Aurora and Naperville, have rushed to amend their ordinances in time for summer [2004].

They have added exemptions that would prevent juveniles from being detained by police if they are out late for a legal activity, such as a religious event or a political rally.

But some municipalities have not acted yet and have suspended their curfew laws in the meantime, and the state has not yet revised its law. The result is that curfew law—and its enforcement—can vary from city to city, creating a legal labyrinth for youths wishing to travel late at night.

Still, many local law enforcement agencies believe a curfew law is a valuable weapon, although there's no data to prove that curfews deter youth crime or protect them from harm.

"[Curfew] is more symbolic than substantive," said Dan Macallair, executive director of the San Francisco-based Center on Juvenile and Criminal Justice. "It allows [police] to appear to be doing something when they are really not."

But law enforcement and city officials insist curfews work.

"Curfew is a powerful tool for getting minors off the streets when they probably should not be there," said Ron O'Neal, an Aurora city attorney.

A Rallying Cry

Curfew became the rallying cry of many cities during the late 1990s as they began to enforce laws that had been on the books for decades. But a number of court challenges raised the question of their constitutionality.

Those included the Indiana case that spurred the recent changes. The Hodgkins v. Peterson case began in 1999 when police arrested Colin Hodgkins, 16, and other teens after they left a restaurant in the Indianapolis area, five minutes past the 11 p.m. curfew. Hodgkins was out late with his parents' permission.

Colin and his friends were handcuffed, required to take breathalyzer and drug tests, and detained for 2½ hours before the families were notified.

The Hodgkins family sued, and a federal district court declared the law unconstitutional. The Indiana General Assembly then amended its law to allow police to arrest minors for curfew violations and allow youths to later prove they were out for legitimate reasons.

The Hodgkinses sued again, arguing that the new law still didn't protect the 1st Amendment rights of young people. The family also argued that the law violated the 14th Amendment by taking away the parents' right to make decisions about what their children can do after curfew hours. The federal appeals court agreed with the first argument, but it left the question of parental rights unanswered.

The rewritten Indiana statute said citations could be issued and teens accused of violating the law could defend themselves later in court. But the court said officers had to give youths a chance to explain their reasons for being out past curfew before a citation is issued.

That's what Elmhurst Deputy Police Chief Jim Doherty has always instructed his officers to do, even though Elmhurst is still revising its law. He said he has always told his officers to enforce curfew by asking questions and using their common sense.

"It was in the officers' discretion not to make that arrest," Doherty said of police in the Hodgkins' case. Laimutis Nargelenas, manager of governmental relations and training for the Illinois Association of Police Chiefs, said they have been advising member departments to follow the court decision even if their cities have not amended the law. Either way, the ruling opens up a minefield of potential lawsuits and further challenges to the law as police officers are expected to decide whether an excuse is valid and whether a youth is telling the truth.

State Rep. John Millner (R-Carol Stream) sponsored an amendment to the Illinois curfew law that has already passed the House and is awaiting action in the Senate.

It would allow minors to legally stay out past curfew if they are attending an official school or religious function or exercising their 1st Amendment rights.

Amending Curfew Ordinances

The city of Chicago was the first Illinois municipality to amend its curfew ordinance, keeping its 10:30 P.M. curfew on weekdays and 11:30 P.M. on weekends. The state and many municipalities enforce an 11 P.M. curfew on weekdays and midnight on weekends.

Following Chicago's lead, Orland Park, Mount Prospect and other suburbs changed their ordinances so they could keep kids off the street who didn't have what the court said were valid reasons for being out.

Cities such as Winfield said they would continue to cite youths for curfew violations under the current state statute. But Winfield Police Chief Douglas Riner said his department has little problem with curfew scofflaws.

The Lake Forest Police Department continued enforcing the law but made officers write curfew violators warnings until the city could "tweak" the ordinance, said Deputy Chief David Field. Their revised law with the exceptions will take effect [July 2004]. . . .

Others, such as the Oak Park Police Department, suspended curfew enforcement until they could pass a law that was constitutional.

"Our attorneys recognized immediately [the need] to suspend active enforcement," said David Powers, communication director for Oak Park. "The court ruling was pretty clear."

Millner's bill also would punish parents who knowingly allow their children to break curfew.

"Many parents don't pay attention to their kids after hours," Millner said. "If they know their kids are out and they don't care, they have to be held accountable."

Parents' rights have become a central question surrounding curfew enforcement, said Kenneth Falk of the Indiana ACLU [American Civil Liberties Union], who argued the Hodgkins case.

Falk is working on another appeal in the case, arguing that parents should be able to let their kids stay out past curfew.

"That's a key to the parental right of the parents fostering their child," Falk said.

CORRECTION: Additional material published July 1, 2004: CORRECTIONS AND CLARIFICATIONS. In a story in Monday's [June 28, 2004] Metro section about inconsistent curfew laws, the police agency that stopped a Naperville Central High School student for speeding was misidentified and the student was incorrectly said to have received a citation for a curfew violation. The student was stopped by Oakbrook Terrace police, not state police, and there was no citation for curfew violation.

6

Teen Curfews Do Not Replace Parental Responsibility

Courtland Milloy

Courtland Milloy is a reporter and columnist for The Washington Post.

The implementation of teen curfew laws, which are intended to control juvenile delinquency, is an attempt to outsource what only compassionate, caring parents can provide: parental responsibility. Although the best circumstances cannot guarantee that a child will grow up to be a responsible teen and adult, irresponsible parenting inevitably fails. Therefore, the education system and government must no longer be blamed for, or expected to remedy, a child's failings or misconduct. Instead, parents must learn what parenting responsibly means, providing guidance and teaching children the consequences of irresponsibility. Teen curfew laws, on the other hand, are not necessary.

When I was growing up in Shreveport, La., juvenile curfews were established by what appeared to us kids as a kind of partnership between our parents and a public utility called Southwestern Electric Power Co. Here's how it worked: On school days, just before the sun went down, a switch would be flipped at SWEPCO, and the streetlights would come on. By parental decree, that was the signal to end whatever fun we were having outdoors and go home.

For those who ignored the lights, another kind of switch got flipped when they eventually showed up. This switch was a tree branch stripped of leaves, and in the hands of an irate mom or dad, it could deliver the jolt of a lightning strike.

As questionable as the practice may have been, the intent was good: to teach that irresponsibility has consequences. And the more responsible we became, our parents assured us, the less likely we were to end up paying the ultimate consequence: In my case, that meant a trip to the state penitentiary at Angola, home of the Big Switch—the one that fired up the electric chair.

Of course, times have changed. These days, spanking your child is out of favor. And you can't put them out of the house. No matter how ugly they act, you can't hit them or deprive them of shelter—unless you want to be arrested and charged with child abuse and neglect. Let me emphasize that the use of corporal punishment probably left many kids with more emotional scars than actual welts. Still, it was better to learn the lessons of responsibility and consequence at home than on the streets. A switch might hurt, but a police baton could kill. And being sent to your room was nothing compared with being locked in a prison cell.

Curfews may be necessary in war-torn cities such as Beirut and Baghdad. What we need here is more caring and compassion.

So, just what is a more-effective way to teach children the principles of responsibility and consequence? In some cities, juvenile curfew laws are among the tools used to control the behavior of troublesome youths. In the District [of Columbia], police are expected next week [in July 2006] to begin enforcing a curfew law that, generally speaking, requires youths 16 or younger to be off the streets by 10 p.m. In other words, what parents used to accomplish with a streetlight and switch is being attempted with searchlights and police sweeps.

Outsourcing Parental Responsibility

But parental responsibility cannot be outsourced. A parent's got to parent. That's all there is to it. And although there is no guarantee that even responsible parents will succeed in raising a child into a responsible adult, the chances are almost nil that an irresponsible parent will succeed.

The fact is, loving, responsible parents are the solution to virtually all that ails our society. But we avoid that reality like the plague. If our children don't learn, we blame the schools. If too many of our children are being arrested, we blame the police. If there aren't enough recreation programs, we blame the mayor. If there are too many guns and drugs on the street, it's the president's fault.

No, it's our fault—if only for expecting that the same government that fails us again and again will somehow change just because we complain, even if we do little else.

Understand this: Nobody takes irresponsible parents seriously—not teachers, not elected officials, not even their own kids. Parents need to learn what it means to be responsible—preferably before becoming parents. Then, maybe we wouldn't resort to having police officers chase our children through the night. And we wouldn't have children being arrested and paying the price of their parents' irresponsibility.

I recently received a copy of an e-mail by Johnny W. Allem, a longtime advocate for addiction treatment in Washington.

He was sharing his impressions of a city conference on substance abuse that was held not long ago.

"Our failure to engage and prepare our young to cope and prosper as adults is a chain of many broken promises," Allem wrote. "Most visible is our broken school system. Less visible is our health, social service and criminal justice systems. Our businesses and churches offer little hope for these citizens of tomorrow."

That is all true. But let's not forget who gives that first ray of hope to the child and who is responsible for sustaining it. In the chain of broken promises that blight a child's life, parents usually provide the first link.

Curfews may be necessary in war-torn cities such as Beirut and Baghdad. What we need here is more caring and compassion.

7

Teen Curfews at Malls Are Effective

Claudia Strage Castaybert

Former journalist Claudia Strage Castaybert is a homemaker.

To end loitering and disruptive behavior, teen curfews at malls are often a last resort. Unruly cliques and threatening groups of teenagers may cause headaches for security, but the teen demographic is the lifeblood of the retail industry. However, at malls where teen curfews have been enforced—on weeknights or during the weekend—the risk was well worth it. Retailers report that customers are left in peace, and those who left to shop elsewhere because of rowdy young crowds return. Though sales initially dip, they bounce back as teens come back with their parents to go shopping. And curfews at malls have other benefits; teens spend more money when accompanied by parents, and some young people even report feeling safer.

It's a relaxed Saturday night at the Metrocenter mall in Jackson, Miss. Shoppers move in and out of stores, arms heavy with bags. They might grab a bite at the food court, and then stroll out to their cars. All in all, a peaceful evening.

But [in 2002], the atmosphere was not so calm. Rowdy teens had overtaken the mall, turning it into a weekend hot spot for wayward youth. The thuggish crowds did more loitering and carousing than spending. "They would intimidate our other customers to the point where they didn't even want to come in the door," says Kymberley Woodard, Coyote Management's director of marketing. Many didn't. They went shopping elsewhere, and before long the mall's vacancy rate [increased] and sales began to suffer.

Now, the only teens you'll see in the Metrocenter on a Friday or Saturday between 3 P.M. and closing are those accompanied by adults. The curfew applies to anyone under 17. Coyote has banned unaccompanied teens from Metrocenter on weekend evenings so adults can visit the mall in peace.

Paying Off

As controversial as the policy may be, it has worked, says Woodard: "From day one it's been paying off." While sales for some retailers slowed right after the curfew started in October [2002], sales began rising again in November [2002] as more adults returned and more parents shopped with their kids.

Metrocenter is not alone. Other city malls are enforcing similar policies. Buffalo-based Pyramid Cos., for example, enforces curfews at two malls it operates in upstate New York: Walden Galleria in Buffalo and Carousel Center in Syracuse. And in Durham, N.C., Northgate Associates' Northgate Mall prohibits teens under 16 to shop without a chaperone weekend evenings.

Curfews are usually a last resort. Some malls, for example, blast classical music over the speakers to chase out disruptive teens who favor more discordant sounds. Coyote tried other measures first, including beefed-up private security and closer ties with the local police. "We even tried a policy of breaking up groups of four or more teens," Woodard says. Still, the problem grew. "We were getting complaints from tenants about the kids loitering," she recalls.

When the company decided to take the extreme step of a curfew, it used focus groups, polled local schools and even conducted a telephone survey of some 350 local residents to help determine whether a curfew was the best way to go. "We wanted to do this thing right," Woodard says.

Because doing the wrong thing can cost developers and their tenants dearly.

"The risk is that for a few bad apples, they (mall owners) are cutting their own throats," says Paco Underbill, a consumer theorist and managing director of Envirosell, a marketing consulting firm. Some teens may represent a security headache, but as a group they are the lifeblood of the retail industry.

Numbering more than 32 million nationwide, shoppers between 12 and 19 years of age spent more than $170 billion last year [2002], which includes their own money and their parents', according to Teenage Research Unlimited, a research firm in Northbrook, Ill.

Teens spend more time in malls than any other age group—an average of about 84 hours every three months compared with 73 hours for 35- to 44-year-olds. Teens are more frequent visitors to the mall, visiting about 50 percent more often than their parents, according to the International Council of Shopping Centers. ICSC defines a teen as someone between 14 years old and 17.

Telling teens they can't shop alone could backfire. "The curfew should be one of the tools in a playbook, but misapplied it will merely push the traffic somewhere else," says Underbill.

While traffic and sales may suffer immediately after a curfew is imposed, retailers say, both pick up quickly as teens return to the mall with adults later on.

Retailers who depend on teen spending are understandably not thrilled with the curfews. "The fact that teenagers can't come in on their own definitely impacts sales," says Kevin Kim, marketing director for Against All Odds, a hip-hop-style retailer and tenant at the Walden Galleria. "A lot of the people the mall was having problems with were our customers," he says. Still, the Moonachie, N.J.-based company, which has 25 stores in New York, New Jersey and Massachusetts, plans to open its biggest store yet in the Galleria's sister mall in Syracuse, the Carousel Center, which also enforces a curfew. "We're working on ideas like sales and other promotions to get customers in earlier in the day or with adult escorts," Kim says.

Despite the downside and controversy of displacing teens on weekend nights, an increasing number of mall owners are finding it worth it to achieve the more shopper-friendly environment that curfews promise. "When you have large groups of teens using abusive language or just being loud, it's intimidating to the other shoppers," says Russ Fulton, Walden Galleria marketing director. Kids under 18 there must be accompanied by someone 21 or older after 4 P.M. on Fridays and Saturdays.

While traffic and sales may suffer immediately after a curfew is imposed, retailers say, both pick up quickly as teens return to the mall with adults later on. Some Metrocenter retailers experienced a dip in business after the October start of the curfew, but "by November and December [2002] traffic and sales were up again," according to Coyote's Woodard.

Traffic was 6 percent higher in November and December after the "Family First" policy was instituted, than in the year earlier period, says Woodard. November sales were 5 percent higher than a year earlier [IN 2001], when there was no curfew, she says. The ICSC benchmark, meanwhile, was flat in November [2002].

In a survey of 120 tenants at the mall, all but about a dozen said they noticed a positive impact on business from Metrocenter's "Family First" program. Shoe and family apparel retail sales were 17 percent higher in November [2002] than a year earlier, according to a report the company prepared to assess the program.

Pyramid has seen positive results as well. "For us the effect has been very good," says Fulton. "The teens we're keeping out probably weren't spending money anyway," he adds. "The ones we have coming with their parents now are truly interested in shopping."

Benefits Beyond Limiting Disturbances

Obliging teens to visit the mall with an adult on weekends can have benefits beyond limiting disturbances. Teens shopping alone spend the least among all age groups per visit, averaging $46.80. But shoppers between 35 and 44 years of age spend about $80 each time they hit the mall, and adults 45 to 54 years old spend $84, the most of all age groups. And they are more likely to whip out the credit card and spend more than their unaccompanied kids would.

What do teens think of curfews? It depends on who you ask. Some are actually relieved: "It's a good thing for our safety because the kids it keeps out might be the sort who pick on other kids," says Kathryn Hupp, a 14-year-old regular at the Mall of America in Bloomington, Minn.

The mall of all malls was the pioneer, introducing a curfew in 1996 when management determined it couldn't handle the estimated influx of 5,000 teens roaming the halls weekend evenings. Thanks to a highly publicized program and dozens of volunteer parents, the program at Mall of America was considered a success. Other malls try to copy it. Meanwhile, teens who "just want to hang out," at the mall, Hupp says, have a choice of several other area shopping centers that don't have curfews.

Not all teens have that option, though. Some experts are concerned that keeping unaccompanied kids out of the mall is choking off an important social venue and may lead them to seek other, less safe options. "Gathering is what teens do," says Roger Blackwell, professor of marketing at the Ohio State University. "They are going to meet up with each other and socialize, and the mall is a much safer and attractive place to be for them than the street corner or a vacant lot."

But for now, in Jackson, Miss., at least, they will have to find places other than the Metrocenter Mall to congregate on weekends. It's "Adults Only" after 3 P.M. Fridays and Saturdays.

8

Teen Curfews at Malls Are Unfair

Clayton High School Globe

The Clayton High School Globe *is the student newspaper of Clayton High School, in Clayton, Missouri.*

Teen curfews at malls unfairly hold youths responsible for disruption, crime, and security problems. Disturbances at malls are related to a larger influx of crowds, not to the limited actions of teens, deeming such restrictions useless. For example, at a mall in Missouri, a 2006 brawl involved two people over twenty-one—not just high school students. The mall also experienced an increase in crime after a public transportation extension opened. Instead of curfews, malls should beef up security to prevent crime and deter disruptive behavior. Shutting teens without chaperones out of malls is not only arbitrary and ineffective, but results in ample revenue losses for retailers.

They may be a year away from graduating high school and they may have their driver licenses but as of Nov. 17 [2006], teens who want to go to St. Louis Mills mall [in Missouri] on Friday and Saturday nights will have to hold mommy's hand.

In order to provide more of a "family night atmosphere" the Mills has created a weekend curfew for customers under age 17, saying that if they wish to be at the mall after 6 p.m., a parent or guardian who is at least 21 must be in accompaniment.

This rule, though adopted in other malls nationwide, such as the Mall of America in Minneapolis, is the first of its kind to appear in St. Louis.

Although St. Louis Mills' decision to implement this rule may directly affect students in Clayton, perhaps we should think twice.

Several weeks ago, around 8:30 p.m. on Nov. 11 [2006], a brawl broke out at the St. Louis Galleria located just miles from Clayton High School. At least one CHS student was involved.

Though Galleria officials assure that there is no curfew at the moment, they are considering different actions for the holiday shopping.

If the Galleria decides that a curfew akin to the one at St. Louis Mills is necessary, neither teens, who amply contribute to a mall's income, nor mall officials would be satisfied with the decision as St. Louis Mills will soon see.

There are about 33.5 million teenagers in the United States today and they are spending more money than ever—an estimated $179 billion for 2006 alone.

The fact is this: teens don't want to hang with their parents on a weekend night. So why would they go to the mall with them?

Shutting teens without parental chaperones out of the shopping mall on the busiest sales nights of the week would make the loss of revenue pretty large.

Besides the fiscal incomprehensibility of the idea of a curfew, the effectiveness of cutting down on fighting is pretty nil. Sticking to the Mills example, with a curfew for those under 17, and transplanting it to the Galleria shows the restriction would not work.

Two of the four people charged with the connection to the Nov. 11 mall altercation where 26 and 21. The other two were 17.

A Hard Rep

It would seem that brawling spans generations and cannot be limited . . . simply to teens although people want to blame teens for making the mall unsafe.

Richmond Heights Police say that though the Galleria incident was isolated, crimes such as car break-ins have shot up at the mall since the opening of the Metrolink extension.

"More people, easier access to the mall from the city and county," Richmond Heights Police Sgt. Marty Votaw said. "Whenever you make easier access and you get larger crowds, you are going to have more crime."

It would seem that larger crowds are the cause of more crime, not the [select] teens.

Though teenagers get a hard rep a lot of the time for being rascals, the majority of us do not go around fighting in shopping malls. The curfew restriction is unfair to those teens who simply go the mall to shop.

However, the problem still lies in what to do about crime at the Galleria and other area malls.

A Fox-2 News poll, on Nov. 15 [2006,] cited that 61 percent of the people they polled avoided malls where violent crime has happened.

Teens who harass customers or behave inappropriately should be asked to leave, but all teens should not be painted with the same broad brush.

Obviously, the Galleria, St. Louis Mills and other malls must do something to counteract violent activity. The solution does not lie in making an arbitrary curfew for teens.

Instead, the Galleria should consider beefing up security. The fact that the Galleria could not locate a brawl beginning in the very visible food court and could not stop if from spreading to the . . . other three levels is ludicrous.

The only conclusion to make is that the mall is under-staffed with its security employees. The better solution is to spend money so more security can patrol the mall.

Also, teens who harass customers or behave inappropriately should be asked to leave but all teens should not be painted with the same broad brush.

Not only do these options offer a very visible reassurance to customers, they are also more fiscally respectable to allow teens to shop and spend their money at the mall on the busiest nights of the week.

And mom and dad won't have to spend their weekend nights holding their teen's hand while they shop.

9

Teen Daytime Curfews Are Effective

Kevin McKeon and Kelly Canally-Brown

Kevin McKeon is commander of criminal investigations at Norristown, Pennsylvania's Police Department. Kelly Canally-Brown is director of community prevention services at Family Services in Norristown.

The increasing rates of truancy and school dropouts are major issues facing school districts and police departments nationwide. Truancy is linked to substance abuse, gang activity, theft, and vandalism. It is also a strong predictor of criminal activity in adulthood. The enforcement of a daytime curfew—integrated with student outreach, parental education, and intervention programs—can effectively reduce truancy and delinquency. For example, the Truancy Abatement Initiative in Norristown, Pennsylvania, decreased unexcused absences of more than half of truant students by 25 percent using a daytime curfew. Addressing this problem stops youths' progression into more serious criminal behavior and prevents school dropouts.

A critical issue facing police departments and school districts across the United States is the increasing incidence of truancy and school dropout. In addition to increasing the likelihood of school failure among minors, truancy has numerous adverse effects on the community, as truant youth often participate in unacceptable or illegal behavior that demands an increasing amount of time from local law enforcement agencies and also contributes to safety concerns among residents in high-crime areas. A 2001 report issued by the Office of Juvenile Justice and Delinquency Prevention, U.S. Department of Justice, found that truancy has been linked to serious delinquent activity in youths and to significant antisocial behavior when these youths become adults. Truancy has been found to be related to substance abuse, gang activity, and involvement in such criminal activities as burglary, aggravated assault, auto theft, and vandalism.

If not addressed, truancy during the adolescent years can have significant negative effects on students, schools, and the community.

The borough of Norristown, located approximately 20 miles northwest of the city of Philadelphia, Pennsylvania, is 3.69 square miles in area and serves as the Montgomery County seat. The daytime population is more than 50,000 and falls to 30,880 at night. According to data from the 2000 U.S. census, Norristown is a diverse community, with a population that is 54 percent white, 35 percent African American, and 11 percent Latino. Norristown consistently evidences the highest rates of domestic violence, substance abuse, child abuse, school dropout, unemployment, inadequate housing, and violent crime in Montgomery County. Although Norristown is demographically small, the community is experiencing "big-city" issues. In 2005 the incidence of violent crime in Norristown increased by 41 percent from the previous year. Robbery went up 59 percent; assaults increased by 87 percent; and arson was up 63 percent from 2004. Homicides, assaults with firearms or other weapons, and other forms of violent crime occur daily in this community. The Norristown Area School District (NASD) has one of the highest incidences of truancy in the state of Pennsylvania.

From the 1999–2000 to the 2005–2006 school year, the NASD experienced a 64.5 percent increase in unexcused absences (from 34,198 in 1999–2000 to 56,322 in 2005–2006). Truant youth are often the perpetrators and victims of crime in Norristown.

If not addressed, truancy during the adolescent years can have significant negative effects on students, schools, and the community. Norristown is no exception to the national norm of increasing truancy rates. To increase school enrollment and attendance of truant students, the Norristown Police Department (NPD) has assembled a variety of community partners to develop a comprehensive, effective approach to truancy enforcement and prevention. Through enforcing Norristown's truancy ordinance and daytime curfew, the NPD is preventing the borough's youths from engaging in daytime juvenile crime and other problem behaviors such as drug use, weapons offenses, and chronic school attendance issues, thus reducing the risk of school dropout and increasing youths' chances for future success.

Swift and vigorous enforcement of the daytime curfew ordinance has considerably decreased the amount of daytime juvenile loitering and reinforced the value that children be in school during school hours.

Truancy Abatement Initiative

In response to the area's many crime problems, the NPD decided to take a forceful stance within the community by implementing numerous community policing and social service strategies. One of the tactics initiated to combat the increasing crime rate was the Norristown Truancy Abatement Initiative.

The NPD and its community partners implemented this plan to achieve the following objectives:

- Replicate a model strategy to intervene with chronic truants

- Address the root causes of truancy

- Stop youths' progression from truancy into more serious and violent behaviors

- Reduce the rates of daytime juvenile crime

- Prevent school dropout

The Norristown approach covers five aspects of the problem in its attempt to reduce truancy.

Prevention: The NPD and its community partners have taken the lead in engaging parents of high-risk youth through outreach and parent education at community and school locations. Using national models, prevention education programs, and a community-developed parent education curriculum, police officers and community partners teach parents about risk factors for youth truancy, school dropout, gang involvement, violence, and other antisocial behaviors.

Timely Intervention: As a part of the partnership, the local school district has developed new policies and procedures to identify truant youth in a timely manner and to notify parents/guardians immediately of any unexcused absence at all grade levels. The procedures developed by the NASD reflect state recommendations of the Pennsylvania Statewide Task Force on School Attendance and Truancy Reduction, which provided guidelines for Pennsylvania school districts regarding implementation of the student achievement and attendance requirements of the federal No Child Left Behind Act of 2001. The NASD issues a letter to a truant student's parents after each unexcused absence. After the third unexcused absence, NASD staff coordinate a school-family conference to discuss the cause of the child's truancy and to agree on a truancy elimination plan (TEP). The TEP is developed in an effort to resolve the truant behavior and will include a review of the appropriateness of the child's educational environment, current academic difficulties, physical or behavioral health issues, and family/environment concerns. The TEP includes the activities that will be undertaken by the school, the parents, and the child to prevent further truancy and can include use of academic and social/health supports from the school and/or community organizations.

Enforcement: A primary objective of the Truancy Abatement Initiative is to return chronically truant youths to school through the coordination and cooperation of local schools, law enforcement officers, and community agencies. NPD officers and the home and school visitors of the NASD (two patrol units) conduct continuous sweeps of the municipality three days per week for four hours per day (between 9 a.m. and 2 p.m.) while school is in session. Strategies used by the truancy abatement patrol unit include apprehending youths who are on the streets during school hours, conducting home-to-home sweeps of youths who are deemed absent without excuse by the NASD home and school visitors, and patrolling areas frequented by truant youths (such as drug houses, parks, or known areas that experience daytime crime). The NPD issues citations to parents of youths apprehended as truant.

In addition, as a support to the Truancy Abatement initiative, the NPD instituted a daytime curfew ordinance. Swift and vigorous enforcement of the daytime curfew ordinance has considerably decreased the amount of daytime juvenile loitering and reinforced the value that children be in school during school hours, increasing the school's enrollment and attendance of high-risk students, which enables these young people to obtain an education and increase their chances of future success.

Follow-up: Citations to appear in court are issued to chronically truant students as well as those truants who fail to follow through on the activities agreed on in their TEP, resulting in additional unexcused absences. Through the NPD partnership, the District Court offers these families alternatives to paying a sizable fine, such as attending a parent education program or participating in counseling or another partnership-sponsored service. Partners in the Truancy Abatement Initiative (law enforcement, school, and community agencies) are present at each District Court hearing for truancy violators. Social services staff and other organizations meet with families after their court hearings to assess their needs for service to prevent future unexcused absences. Agency representatives conduct on-site intake assessments for counseling services at this time. Other services include drug, alcohol, and mental health screenings; housing and mentoring programs; and after-school resources. Effective coordination with the District Court has been integral to the success of the Norristown Truancy Abatement Initiative.

Changing Community Norms: Many Norristown youths view a high school diploma as an unachievable goal (28.5 percent of Norristown's adult population has not completed high school). A primary emphasis of the Truancy Abatement Initiative is to change the community norms regarding school commitment and violence, as well as to increase the value of education. Strategies developed to change community norms have encompassed environmental, social-marketing, and community education/outreach.

Evaluation Plan

There are many indicators of success that the NPD and its community partners review on a regular basis to determine the short-term and long-term effectiveness of their truancy intervention plan, with the primary goal of keeping students in school:

- Long- and short-term changes in attendance among students referred for intervention

- Improved average daily attendance rate in the schools the intervention subjects attend

- Timeliness of intervention and the effect on students' attendance

- Characteristics of the students whose attendance improved

- Extent to which teachers assess the factors that lead to attendance problems for a student

- Process measures, including the following:

     Number of students brought to school

     Number of parent contacts

     Number of TEPs developed for any student having three or more unexcused absences

     Number of behavior management sessions attended by students

     Decreases in Uniform Crime Report Part I crimes

     Decreases in daytime juvenile crimes

Tangible Achievements

When comparing data from two equal time periods—March 2006, when the initial activities of the Truancy Abatement Initiative were undertaken, and March 2007, after full implementation—the NPD observed two significant outcomes attributed to the initiative and the related daytime curfew. Major crimes decreased by 10 percent, and arrests for major crimes decreased by 15 percent. When comparing annual figures for 2006 with those of 2007, the NPD reported an 11 percent decrease in major crimes and a 36 percent decrease in arrests for major crimes (as of December 2007). The decreases follow several years of a trend of increasing rates of Part I crimes.

In addition, the Truancy Abatement Initiative has achieved the following outcomes:

- Comparing marking period attendance records before and after court involvement, 55 percent of truant youths decreased their number of unexcused absences by greater than 25 percent.

- Of parent education and counseling participants, 89 percent increased their knowledge of the critical risk factors for youth violence, gang involvement, and truancy.

- Of the same group, 85 percent reported an increased ability to prevent or reduce youth at-risk behavior.

- The overall rate of unexcused absences for the NASD decreased by 27 percent from the 2005–2006 (55,136 absences) to the 2007–2008 (40,462 absences) school year.

A primary emphasis of this initiative has been on engaging the appropriate community partners to change the community norms related to school commitment and violence as well as increasing the value of education. In addition to providing direct services to high-risk youth and their families, the combined collaborative efforts aim to affect how business owners, parents, youths, and other community stakeholders reinforce school attendance and high school graduation rates.

This partnership reflects the tremendous impact communities can have with a collective, coordinated effort. The activities of the NPD Truancy Abatement Initiative can be replicated with diverse community partners willing to direct resources in a coordinated manner.

10

Teen Daytime Curfews Target Minority and Disadvantaged Youths

Sarah Viren

Sarah Viren is a Texas-based journalist who has reported for The Houston Chronicle *and* The Galveston County Daily News.

Law enforcement officials and schools credit daytime teen curfews with cutting down burglaries and petty crime, reducing truancy, and preventing teens from being victimized. However, home-school and civil liberties groups contend that daytime teen curfews are disproportionately enforced in minority and poor areas, meaning some youths are more likely than others to receive curfew citations. Parents also oppose such laws when they are enforced in close proximity to campuses, and experts cite a lack of definitive proof supporting the effectiveness of curfews in reducing crime and juvenile delinquency. Because of the lack of resources to impose these laws equally, curfews can be subject to selective enforcement.

More than an hour after the first bell Friday morning, Mike Flores spotted a teenager climbing from his car and heading to class at Madison High School.

"Where you going, man?" hollered Flores, an officer with the Houston Police Department's Southwest Patrol. "You know you're in violation of the curfew. You got to be here on time."

Sarah Viren, "Youths Aren't the Only Ones Opposing Curfews: County's Decision Against Daytime Law Comes Amid Concerns Over Intrusion and Enforcement," *Houston Chronicle*, September 16, 2007. Copyright © 2007 Houston Chronicle. Republished with permission of Houston Chronicle, conveyed through Copyright Clearance Center, Inc.

He was talking about the daytime curfew law, a Houston city regulation that, in essence, lets police stop any youngster on the street during a school day and ask: "What's up?"

Law enforcement and schools tend to like the law, which they believe cuts down on burglaries and petty crime, reduces truancy and helps protect teens from becoming victims themselves. But home-school and civil liberties groups have consistently lobbied against curfews, and some experts say there is no definitive proof they work. Last week [in September 2007], Harris County commissioners rejected a request from prosecutors to extend daytime curfews to unincorporated areas; County Judge Ed Emmett called the measure too intrusive.

In Houston, where being young and on the streets during school hours has long been a ticketable offense, curfews soldier on, reviewed and re-approved every three years. Police officers from certain neighborhoods say they've recorded drops in some crimes after cracking down on youths playing hooky. But an initial review of the curfew law after its adoption in 1991 showed that daytime crimes by juveniles actually increased after school-hour curfews took effect.

And, in what critics call a common problem with these laws, Houston's curfew appears to be enforced more frequently in certain areas of town—particularly the southwest side— meaning some youths may be more likely to be ticketed.

"[Police] tend to target a specific area because of crime, and they go into that area to go after curfew violations," said Ken Adams, a professor of health and public affairs at the University of Central Florida, who has studied curfew laws.

In his 2003 review of major research on the issue, Adams found that curfews overall—both night and daytime—haven't been shown to reduce crime. And, in at least one study he reviewed, from Cincinnati, truancy actually went up, rather than down, when a daytime curfew took effect.

Texas law requires students younger than 18, with a few exceptions, to be in school. But enforcement is traditionally left to school districts, which hire truancy officers to track un-excused absences before taking a child to court. Curfew laws, however, get the police involved, allowing them to slap a mis-demeanor charge on nearly any student caught on the street, without an excuse, during daytime hours.

Youths, Parents Dispute Law

In 2006, Houston police issued more than 3,100 such tickets. They've written nearly 2,000 so far this year [2007].

One of those was for Rigoberto Flores, 14, who got a ticket in May after stopping at Jack in the Box for breakfast before class at an alternative school on the city's southwest side. As Flores walked up to campus, he said he saw several police officers outside ticketing tardy students.

"They were issuing tickets to everybody," he said, after appearing in Municipal Court this week in a clean white shirt and pressed khakis. Judge David Fraga, who handles nearly all curfew tickets, allowed him to attend a class on the dangers of skipping school in lieu of paying the curfew fine, which can range from $180 to $225.

What we've seen in most, if not all, cities that have curfew laws is that police will enforce the curfew in minority and poor neighborhoods.

Most youths filing into that court last week said they found the laws unfair, and some parents complained about tickets handed out so close to campuses. But police working the streets call them a godsend.

Last school year [2006], after seeing a rise in burglaries and after the fatal drive-by shooting of a student just outside Westbury High School's fenced campus, the city's Southwest Patrol formed a unit dedicated to those cutting class, said Lt. Larry Crowson.

After the first 75 days of ticketing skippers, violent crimes and burglaries in the Westbury neighborhood declined about 16 percent from the previous 75-day period, said Crowson, who acknowledged limitations to the analysis, which didn't compare the same times of the year.

On the Prowl

The program worked well enough, though, that it is continuing this year [2007], with at least four officers on the streets each day ticketing those who skip. That was Flores' job on Friday when he circled each of this district's larger schools, looking for students sneaking off campus or arriving late to class. The boy he spotted outside Madison High School was 17—too old for a curfew ticket—but Flores gave him one for driving without a license instead.

At the Eastside police station, near Chavez and Milby high schools, two officers are similarly dedicated to catching truants. These sections of town are apparent hot spots for daytime curfew citations. Although any officer can issue a ticket for skipping school, tickets seem to come predominantly from these areas, according to a *Houston Chronicle* analysis of citations from 2006 to date [2007].

Minorities Often Ticketed

Uneven enforcement is a big rallying cry for critics of curfew laws.

"What we've seen in most, if not all, cities that have curfew laws is that police will enforce the curfew in minority and poor neighborhoods," said Alex Koroknay-Palicz, executive director for the National Youth Rights Association, which fights curfews.

In Houston, more tickets are issued to blacks and Hispanics, but minorities are also an overwhelming majority on Houston Independent School District campuses. Last year [2006], more than half of all curfew tickets went to blacks, who make up about 30 percent of HISD students; 36 percent went to Hispanics, who comprise 58 percent of HISD, and Anglos, who comprise nearly 9 percent of the district's students, were ticketed 6 percent of the time, according to state and police data.

Still, Bellaire Assistant Police Chief Byron Holloway said uneven enforcement is one reason he's hesitant about curfew laws. His tiny city, tucked within the Houston metropolis, has no juvenile curfew restrictions. That means Bellaire High School students may freely walk the streets during the school day, although schools could still get them for truancy.

"This is the deal with curfew laws: They can be subject to selective enforcement," he said, "because you seldom have the resources to equally enforce it."

11

Teens Should Have Driving Curfews

Allan F. Williams

Allan F. Williams is a highway safety consultant and the former chief scientist of the Insurance Institute of Highway Safety in Arlington, Virginia.

Drivers who are sixteen years old represent the age group that has the highest crash risk of all drivers. The type of crash most often attributed to teen drivers—off-the-road, single-vehicle collisions involving speeding, distractions, or risk-taking—are linked to immaturity and driver inexperience. Graduated licensing is a solution to this public health problem. It imposes curfews that restrict sixteen-year-old drivers from driving at night without adult supervision, or during an unendorsed activity, that phase out as driving experience is gained. In states where night driving restrictions are enforced, crash rates among the youngest drivers have been dramatically reduced. Parents also widely support driving curfew laws, and teen drivers eventually adapt to these measures.

The Insurance Institute for Highway Safety is a nonprofit research and communications organization that identifies ways to reduce motor vehicle crashes and crash losses. I am the Institute's chief scientist, and I am writing to address the issue of graduated licensing for young drivers. This is an area

Allan F. Williams, "Young Drivers and Graduated Licensing: Statement Before the Transportation Committee, State of Hawaii House of Representatives," Insurance Institute for Highway Safety, February 7, 2003. Reproduced by permission. http://www.iihs.org/laws/testimony/pdf/testimony_afw_020703.pdf.

of special interest to the Institute. We have conducted research on the young driver problem for more than 20 years and published more than 50 articles on this topic in professional journals.

The young driver problem is well recognized and acknowledged. Less recognized is that the age group most affected by licensing policies—16-year-olds—has by far the highest crash risk of drivers of any age. Nationally, the crash risk per mile driven by 16-year-olds is nearly three times that of 18–19-year-olds and 10 times the risk of drivers ages 30–59. The problem is that 16-year-olds, as a group, are inexperienced, and they are the youngest and most immature group holding licenses. The crash type most often associated with teenage drivers, especially 16-year-olds, is a single-vehicle, run-off-the-road collision involving speeding and multiple teenage passengers—the very type of crash often caused by immaturity and inexperience behind the wheel.

The methods we have relied on so far to try to reduce injuries associated with young drivers have not worked. Driver education is insufficient. Tougher penalty systems for young drivers, by themselves, have limited effects. States now are turning to graduated licensing as a way to cope with this major public health problem.

In the United States we typically have offered a quick and easy path to a full-privilege license at a very young age—a policy that has allowed the combined effects of driving inexperience and youthfulness to take their toll. In a graduated system, full privileges are phased in so that beginners get their initial driving experience in lower risk settings. They gain on-the-road experience but are protected while doing so, first in a supervised learning phase and then in an intermediate licensing phase during which unsupervised driving is not allowed in high-risk settings—for example, late at night or with other teens in the car. Progress through these stages without incurring traffic violations or crashes leads to full-privilege licensure. The phase-in process takes some time, so young people are not only more experienced but somewhat older and more mature when they attain full privileges.

Driving at night is a high-risk activity for people of all ages, especially the very youngest drivers.

To most people, graduated licensing makes sense. After all, driving is such a complex skill that it cannot be learned overnight or in a few short weeks. It makes sense to employ a type of apprenticeship system for learners, especially because the consequences of driver error and misjudgment can be lethal.

Since 1996, all but a handful of states have adopted some form of graduated licensing. These systems vary substantially in terms of the provisions and duration of the licensing stages and other features—variations that are to be expected as jurisdictions adapt the idea of a graduated system to their own needs and preferences. On the other hand, such variations often create difficulty in jurisdictions where graduated systems are under consideration and policymakers do not necessarily know which features their own systems should include. To address this, the Insurance Institute for Highway Safety and the Traffic Injury Research Foundation of Canada have developed "A Blueprint for Graduated Licensing in North America," which summarizes and assesses progress with graduated systems through 2002. This document also provides recommendations for graduated systems based on scientific research and on what such systems are intended to accomplish.

Night Driving Restrictions

Driving at night is a high-risk activity for people of all ages, especially the very youngest drivers. This is why night driving restrictions are included in 36 graduated licensing laws. We know such restrictions work because a few states have curtailed young people's night driving since at least the 1960s.

For example, New York's restriction (9 P.M. to 5 A.M.) was established before 1970, and Pennsylvania's (midnight-5 A.M.) took effect sometime before 1977. Both restrictions apply to 16-year-olds and to 17-year-olds who have not taken driver education. Although many teenagers say they sometimes violate these restrictions, surveys indicate good overall compliance.

To the extent that restrictions cut down on driving at night, they reduce crashes. And the reductions are dramatic—a 62 percent crash reduction during restricted hours in New York, according to a 1984 study, and a 69 percent reduction in Pennsylvania. Although the percentage reduction in New York is smaller, the total number of crashes averted is much greater than in Pennsylvania because New York's restriction covers the 9 P.M. to midnight hours, a time when many crashes involving young drivers occur. The same study found no evidence of spillover effects to unrestricted hours. Nor were there offsetting increases in injuries to 16-year-old passengers, pedalcyclists, or pedestrians during restricted hours.

The question is often asked, how can police enforce night driving restrictions? In reality, parents are the chief enforcers, and they overwhelmingly favor night driving restrictions. In states without such restrictions, parents want them enacted, and where nighttime restrictions exist parents are even more likely to endorse them. For example, 94 percent of parents of graduating seniors in New York State said they favor the 9 P.M. to 5 A.M. restriction. Parents generally approve of graduated licensing, too. In the absence of state requirements, most parents set up their own rules about where, when, and with whom their children can travel. However, it is much easier for parents to manage this difficult period if the state imposes sensible requirements for phasing in full driving privileges.

As might be expected, young people are not fond of driving restrictions that apply solely to them, although they do understand the rationale for such restrictions and adapt to them over time. For example, when 17–18-year-olds in New York and Pennsylvania were asked if they favor "some kind of night driving curfew for beginning teenage drivers," 80 percent in Pennsylvania and 67 percent in New York said they favor curfews.

It is important to recognize that these restrictions do not ban all driving at night. Driving under adult supervision is allowed, and all states allow unsupervised driving at night that is considered essential. For example, New York allows driving to work or school, and Pennsylvania allows driving to work or while performing volunteer fire department duties. The idea is to restrict high-risk recreational driving without hindering young people's engagement in purposeful activities. Variations are to be expected in terms of what states consider essential and thus exempt from the restrictions.

Driving with Passengers

Another major risk factor for teenage drivers is the presence of passengers, especially teen passengers. For older drivers, passenger presence either has no effect on crash risk or decreases it, but for young drivers passengers greatly magnify the risk. That is, teenagers' already high crash risk when driving alone increases dramatically when passengers are added. This effect is present both at night and during the day and is heightened if the passengers are teenagers—the more teens in the car the greater the risk. A recent study in Canada found that with two or more passengers, the crash risk for male and female teenage drivers was about five times as high as when driving alone.

The reasons are obvious. Teenage passengers create distractions for drivers who are inexperienced to start with and who need to be paying full attention to the driving task. Plus the presence of peers in the car often induces young drivers to take risks. This is why 24 states have introduced passenger limitations as part of their graduated systems.

Effectiveness of Graduated Licensing

The North American graduated systems of the 1990s are so new that evidence of their effectiveness only now is beginning to accumulate—and the evidence is positive. Graduated licensing systems have been shown to be effective in New Zealand and Canada. Evaluations in several U.S. states have also shown positive effects. Florida enacted the first of the modern U.S. graduated systems, featuring a six-month learner's stage and night driving restrictions until age 18. A recent study found a 9 percent reduction in injury crashes among 15–17-year-olds during the first full year of this system, which translates to the prevention of 1,167 injury crashes. Studies in North Carolina, Ohio, and Michigan have found even more positive reductions in crashes, between 20 and 30 percent.

The question is not whether graduated licensing is effective. It is, and the only question is precisely how effective. Of course, such licensing systems are not panaceas. There will still be a problem because teenagers will still be relatively young and inexperienced when they get their licenses. Besides, compliance with restrictions will not be universal. At the same time, graduating licensing represents a giant step forward in addressing this major public health problem.

12

Enforcing Teen Driving Curfews May Be Problematic

Magdalene Perez

Magdalene Perez is a staff writer for The Advocate, *the daily newspaper of Stamford, Connecticut.*

According to driving safety advocates, night driving curfews are needed to remove teen drivers from dangerous—and potentially illegal—situations and to get parents directly involved in monitoring their children's behavior. However, enforcing such restrictions may burden police departments. Measures to prevent driving teens from being profiled based on appearances—such as identification stickers and checkpoints—have met with community opposition or are costly and time-consuming to implement. Additionally, graduated driver licensing laws—which impose restrictions on beginning and intermediate teen drivers—are commonly underenforced. Nonetheless, law enforcement officials are hopeful that curfews and tougher penalties will curb tragic accidents involving young people behind the wheel.

When a tougher teen driving law takes effect Aug. 1, the burden of enforcing it will fall squarely on police.

And in a state where statistics show current teen driving restrictions are under-enforced, legislators are asking state and local police to enforce the new law without extra money or a clear means of identifying teen drivers.

"Departments don't have resources laying around," said Glastonbury Police Chief Thomas Sweeney. "There's an assumption that you can keep stacking laws on police departments and that they're going to be able to enforce them."

The new law, signed by Gov. M. Jodi Rell in April, gives the typical trooper or patrol officer more to think about—and in some cases do—when pulling over a teenage driver.

It will extend passenger restrictions for 16- and 17-year-olds and move the nighttime curfew to 11 p.m. from midnight.

Neil Dougherty, a traffic officer in Glastonbury, got a taste of the new mandates recently, when his boss handed him a four-page summary of the law, which he stuck behind the sun visor in his patrol car.

The first item on the list, titled "48-Hour License Suspension for Certain Violations," is sure to have the biggest impact on police. The provision requires officers to immediately seize the license of teen drivers for violating passenger or curfew restrictions, or for more serious offenses such as driving 20 mph over the speed limit or more, driving under the influence of alcohol or drugs, reckless driving or racing. Officers must hold the temporarily suspended license for 48 hours until the teen and a parent or guardian signs for it.

For teen driving safety advocates, the provision is important because it removes the teenager from a situation where he is breaking the law, and it gets parents involved immediately.

Police said they are glad that it puts parents in the picture, but they also recognize the law means officers will be spending more time calling parents and in some cases driving teenagers home.

"It's not a simple law like speeding," said Dougherty, who has been patrolling for eight years. "The whole law is really labor intensive."

Profiling

The issue of how to identify teen drivers is a touchy one.

A plan to require cars driven by teenagers to have stickers identifying them was supported by police chiefs across the state. But many parents and other Connecticut adults didn't agree. When the governor's office conducted a statewide poll of 807 adults in January, only 38 percent of parents and 43 percent of other adults supported teen identification stickers. In the legislature, the measure was rejected for lack of popular support and cost concerns.

"There was a lot of concern among parents that if a kid had a sticker like that they could be profiled or victims of discrimination," Farmington Police Chief James Rio said.

Both statistics and anecdotal evidence suggest that restrictions on teenage drivers, called graduated driver licensing, or GDL, laws, have been largely under-enforced since they were first introduced in 2004.

Today the conundrum remains. How can police enforce restrictions on teen drivers without knowing which drivers are under 18? Police and the chief state's attorney's office agree that officers cannot single out young drivers because of their appearance.

"We can't just stop a car because a person looks underage and they have a passenger in the car," Rio said.

Unless police departments set up costly and time-consuming police checkpoints near schools or during certain hours, many officers are likely to continue approaching passenger restrictions and curfew laws the way they often do now—as "secondary" infractions, violations that police tack to the "primary" reason for a stop, such as speeding or running a red light, police said. That approach, which avoids profiling, is the proper way to enforce teen driving restrictions, Susan Marcu Naide of the chief state's attorney's office said.

Glastonbury's Chief Sweeney said it is a trade-off the public should be willing to accept if they do not want to give police a visual cue to identify teen drivers.

"Don't come back in a year or two and be distressed by the fact that it's being treated as secondary enforcement," Sweeney said.

Soft on Teens

Both statistics and anecdotal evidence suggest that restrictions on teenage drivers, called graduated driver licensing, or GDL, laws, have been largely under-enforced since they were first introduced in 2004. In 2005, just 262 teen drivers statewide—or about an average of 1.5 per town—were convicted of violating either passenger restriction laws, curfew or both, according to the state Department of Motor Vehicles. That number rose to 600 in 2006 before dropping slightly to 549—an average of about 3.2 convictions per town—in 2007.

"We under-enforce it right now. There's no doubt about it," Rio said. As a member of the governor's teen driving task force, Rio heard parents, teens and driving instructors all say police have been soft on teens in the past.

"We got a lot of anecdotal stories of instances where police officers have stopped kids and either did not recognize that they were in violation of GDL laws or took a very light approach," Rio said.

"I want to get officers in the mind-set that we're going to enforce all the motor vehicle laws," he added. "It's not an incidental thing."

Rio pointed to the enforcement of teen driving laws in Massachusetts as a good example of how "proactive" enforcement can be done. There, police conduct "educational stings" at high schools, issuing warnings to teens who are not in compliance with passenger restriction laws and rewarding those who are with coupons for pizza, lollipops or key chains, according to a spokeswoman for the state Registry of Motor

Vehicles. Only the lollipops are paid for by the registry; the pizza and key chains are donated by AAA and the state Executive Office of Public Safety, respectively.

But there are differences between the two states. In Massachusetts, the state employs 41 compliance officers who help coordinate enforcement and educational stings. And police aren't required to immediately seize a teen's license, meaning they are less likely to get bogged down contacting parents when they issue a citation.

William Seymour, a state DMV spokesman, said his department, law enforcement organizations, the chief state's attorney's office, the state DOT and the federal National Highway Traffic Safety Administration have been meeting regularly to "put together a first-ever graduated driver licensing enforcement program in Connecticut." Seymour also said the state may be able to get federal funds to help with teen driving law enforcement.

Ultimately, local and state police hope the tough penalties for teen drivers—first-time suspensions of 30 days for using a cellphone while driving, violating passenger restrictions or curfew; 60 days for speeding; six months for reckless driving or racing; a year for drinking and driving—will curb the types of tragic accidents that have focused attention on teen driving over the past year.

"I think it's going to work because, No. 1, it's severe," said Lt. Clanford Pierce, a state trooper based in Westbrook. "At that age, a car means everything to these kids."

Teen driving laws that take effect Aug. 1 will require police to seize the licenses of 16- and 17-year-old drivers who:

- Violate driving restrictions or curfew

- Drive 20 mph or more above the speed limit

- Drive under the influence of alcohol or drugs

- Drive recklessly

- Race on a public highway

Organizations to Contact

The editors have compiled the following list of organizations concerned with the issues debated in this book. The descriptions are derived from materials provided by the organizations. All have publications or information available for interested readers. The list was compiled on the date of publication of the present volume; the information provided here may change. Be aware that many organizations take several weeks or longer to respond to inquiries, so allow as much time as possible.

American Civil Liberties Union (ACLU)
125 Broad Street, 18th Floor, New York, NY   10004
(212) 549-2500
Web site: www.aclu.org

The ACLU is a national organization that works to defend Americans' civil rights as guaranteed by the U.S. Constitution. It works to protect students' rights regarding issues such as freedom of speech and curfew laws. Stand Up with the ACLU focuses on civil liberties issues with a youth perspective, including a comic strip series and podcasts.

Americans for a Society Free from Age Restrictions (ASFAR)
P.O. Box 11358, Chicago, IL   60611-0358
Web site: www.asfar.org

ASFAR is an organization dedicated to protecting and advancing the legal civil rights of youth. ASFAR fights the voting age, curfew laws, and other laws that limit the freedom of young people. The association publishes position papers on youth rights and issues regarding age-based restrictions.

Justice Policy Institute (JPI)
1003 K Street, NW, Suite 500, Washington, DC   20001
(202) 558-7974
e-mail: info@justicepolicy.org
Web site: www.justicepolicy.org

Since 1997, JPI has worked to enhance the public dialog on incarceration through accessible research, public education, and communications advocacy. Its areas of research and numerous publications and fact sheets cover issues in juvenile justice, delinquency, and gangs, with an emphasis on alternatives to incarceration.

National Youth Rights Association (NYRA)
1101 Fifteenth Street, NW, Suite 200, Washington, DC   20005
(202) 296-2992 ext. 131
Web site: www.youthrights.org

NYRA is a youth-led national nonprofit organization dedicated to fighting for the civil rights and liberties of young people. NYRA has a total of more than seven thousand members in all fifty states and chapters from coast to coast. It seeks to lower the voting age, lower the drinking age, repeal curfew laws, and protect student rights.

Office of Juvenile Justice and Delinquency Prevention (OJJDP)
U.S. Department of Justice, Washington, DC   20531
(202) 307-5911
Web site: http://ojjdp.ncjrs.org

OJJDP provides national leadership and resources to prevent and respond to juvenile delinquency. It supports community efforts to develop effective programs and improve the juvenile justice system. Publications available at its Web site include "Domestic Assaults by Juvenile Offenders," "The Girls Study Group—Charting the Way to Delinquency Prevention for Girls," and "Juvenile Transfer Laws: An Effective Deterrent to Delinquency?"

National School Safety Center (NSSC)
141 Duesenberg Drive, Suite 11, Westlake Village, CA   91362
(805) 373-9977 • fax: (805) 373-9277
Web site: www.schoolsafety.us

NSSC serves as an advocate for safe, secure, and peaceful schools worldwide and as a catalyst for the prevention of school crime and violence. It provides school communities and their school safety partners with quality information, resources, consultation, and training services. The center's publications include *School Discipline Notebook* and *Student Searches and the Law*.

SoundOut
P.O. Box 6185, Olympia, WA   98507-6185
(360) 753-2686 • fax: (360) 528-2350
e-mail: info@soundout.org
Web site: www.soundout.org

SoundOut promotes student voice in school through research, training, and resource sharing. Its systemic approaches to whole-school reform emphasize practical, considerable, and holistic roles for students as partners in learning and leadership throughout education. Its publications include the *Meaningful Student Involvement Series* and articles from a student point of view.

Youth Crime Watch of America (YCWA)
9200 South Dadeland Boulevard, Suite 417, Miami, FL   33156
(305) 670-2409 • fax: (305) 670-3805
Web site: www.ycwa.org

YCWA is a nonprofit, student-led organization that promotes crime and drug prevention programs in communities and schools throughout the United States. Member-students at the elementary and secondary level help raise others' awareness concerning youth issues and the importance of education. Strategies include organizing student assemblies and patrols, conducting workshops, and challenging students to become personally involved in preventing crime and violence.

Bibliography

Books

Robert Agnew   *Juvenile Delinquency: Causes and Control* (3rd ed.). New York: Oxford University Press, 2008.

Clemens Bartollas and Stuart J. Miller   *Voices in the Juvenile Justice System.* Upper Saddle River, NJ: Prentice Hall, 2008.

Maureen J. Hinds   *You Have a Right to Know Your Rights: What Teens Should Know,* Issues in Focus Today Series. Berkeley Heights, NJ: Enslow, 2005.

Thomas A. Jacobs   *Teens Take It to Court: Young People Who Challenged the Law—And Changed Your Life.* Minneapolis, MN: Free Spirit, 2006.

Rob Long   *Yeah Right! Adolescents in the Classroom (Building Success Through Better Behavior).* London, UK: David Fulton, 2005.

R. Scott Ryder and Preston Elrod   *Juvenile Justice: A Social, Historical, and Legal Perspective (2nd ed.).* Sudbury, MA: Jones and Bartlett, 2005.

Elizabeth S. Scott and Laurence Steinberg   *Rethinking Juvenile Justice.* Cambridge, MA: Harvard University Press, 2008.

Lynn S. Urban   *The Deterrent Effects of Curfews: An Evaluation of Juvenile Probationers.* El Paso, TX: LFB Scholarly Publishing, 2007.

Periodicals

Teresa Ann Boeckel   "Curfew's Mixed Reviews: Some Argue that Daytime Provisions Aren't Necessary Because of Truancy Laws," *McClatchy-Tribune Business News,* April 20, 2008.

Caitlin Carpenter   "For Teens, It's Curfew Time . . . at the Mall," *Christian Science Monitor,* June 6, 2007.

Brian Johnson   "Driving While Young: Why the City's Curfew Isn't All That," *Jackson Free Press,* October 12, 2005.

Judy Keen   "Malls' Night Restrictions on Teens Paying Off," *USA Today,* March 15, 2007.

Joseph Kellard   "The Anti-Self-Responsibility Movement," *Capitalism Magazine,* August 22, 2004.

Sean McCollum   "Mall Curfews: Teen Discrimination?" *Literary Cavalcade,* January 2005.

James McKinney   "Curfews: A New Crime-Fighting Tool," *Time,* September 11, 2008.

Anusha Mohan and Molly Henningsen — "Teen Time Check: Curfews Can Be a Sticking Point Between Parents and Teens," *Contra Costa Times*, February 9, 2006.

Jennifer Morron — "Teen Curfew?" *Gotham Gazette*, March 2006.

Jayne O'Donnell — "Deadly Teen Auto Crashes Show a Pattern," *USA Today*, March 1, 2005.

Cris Prystay — "Teens Out of Control," *Far Eastern Economic Review*, April 1, 2004.

Betsey Taylor — "Malls Try Teen Curfews to Draw Shoppers," *Washington Post*, April 5, 2007.

George Wilson — "Misplaced Punishment," *Washington Informer*, August 3–9, 2006.

Kevin A. Wilson — "Focus on Teen Drivers Bears Fruit," *AutoWeek*, September 8, 2008.

Anthony E. Wolf — "Sorry, You Can't Stop Teenage Snark," *Globe and Mail*, November 25, 2008.

Index